T0215339

Research for Policy

Studies by the Netherlands Council for Government Policy

Series Editors
J. E. J. (Corien) Prins, WRR, Scientific Council for Government Policy,
The Hague, Zuid-Holland, The Netherlands
F. W. A. (Frans) Brom, WRR, Scientific Council for Government Policy,
The Hague, Zuid-Holland, The Netherlands

The Netherlands Scientific Council for Government Policy (WRR) is an independent strategic advisory body for government policy in the Netherlands. It advises the Dutch government and Parliament on long-term strategic issues that are of great importance for society. The WRR provides science-based advice aimed at: opening up new perspectives and directions, changing problem definitions, setting new policy goals, investigating new resources for problem-solving and enriching the public debate.

The studies of the WRR do not focus on one particular policy area, but on cross-cutting issues that affect future policymaking in multiple domains. A long-term perspective complements the day-to-day policymaking, which often concentrates on issues that dominate today's policy agenda.

The WRR consists of a Council and an academic staff who work closely together in multidisciplinary project teams. Council members are appointed by the King, and hold academic chairs at universities, currently in fields as diverse as economics, sociology, law, public administration and governance, health and water management. The WRR determines its own work programme, as well as the content of its publications. All its work is externally reviewed before publication.

The Research for Policy Series
In this series, we publish internationally relevant studies of the Netherlands Scientific Council for Government Policy. Many of the cross-cutting issues that affect Dutch policymaking, also challenge other Western countries or international bodies. By publishing these studies in this international open access scientific series, we hope that our analyses and insights can contribute to the policy debate in other countries.

About the Editors
Corien Prins is Chair of the WRR and Professor of Law and Information Technology at Tilburg Law School (Tilburg University).

Frans Brom is Council secretary and director of the WRR office. He also is Professor of Normativity of Scientific Policy Advice at the Ethics Institute of Utrecht University.

More information about this series at http://www.springer.com/series/16390

Erik Schrijvers • Corien Prins • Reijer Passchier

Preparing for Digital Disruption

Erik Schrijvers
Senior Research Fellow
Netherlands Scientific Council for
Government Policy
The Hague, The Netherlands

Corien Prins
Chair and Member of the Council
Netherlands Scientific Council for
Government Policy
The Hague, The Netherlands

Reijer Passchier
Assistant Professor
Leiden University
Leiden, The Netherlands

ISSN 2662-3684 ISSN 2662-3692 (electronic)
Research for Policy
ISBN 978-3-030-77837-8 ISBN 978-3-030-77838-5 (eBook)
https://doi.org/10.1007/978-3-030-77838-5

This Springer imprint is published by the registered company Springer Nature Switzerland AG
The registered company address is: Gewerbestrasse 11, 6330 Cham, Switzerland

Persons Consulted

Employer and/or position at the time of the interview
L.F.M. van den Aarsen, Ministry of Infrastructure and Water Management
J.C.J.H. Aerts, Vrije Universiteit Amsterdam
E.S.M. Akerboom, National Police
A.J. Akkermans, Vrije Universiteit Amsterdam
N. Aland, National Coordinator for Security and Counterterrorism
J. van Alphen, Delta Programme Commissioner
P. Antenbrink, The Netherlands Court of Audit
H. Arnold, Centre for Crime Prevention and Security
H. Backx, GGD GHOR Nederland
R. Bakker, City of Rotterdam
E. Beekman, Academic Medical Centre
A.J.M. van Bellen, ECP, Platform for the Information Society
R. Bening, ING
R.A. Boin, Leiden University
W.H. van Boom, Leiden University
M.P. Boots, Ministry of General Affairs
P.L.J. Bos, Utrecht Safety Region
T. Brinkman, Association of Insurers
E. Bronsdijk, City of Rotterdam
V. Bruggeman, Environmental Law and Policy Consulting
G.W. van der Burg, Public Prosecution Service of the Netherlands
M. Coenders, City of Rotterdam
M.T.A. Coenders, Utrecht University
C. Contino, Victim Support Fund
F. Dezeure, Freddy Dezeure BVBA
M. van Dorssen, Berenschot BV
H.L. Duijnhoven, TNO
J.F.E. Farwerck, KPN
M. Faure, Maastricht University
P. van der Feltz, Google Nederland

E. Fledderus, Surf
M. Groenendijk, Evides Water Company
I.M. Haisma, Sim-ci/Alliander
T. Hartlief, Utrecht University
P. Hartman, Riskfit Innovation
E. van den Heuvel, Cyber Security Raad (Cyber Security Council)
L. Holterman, Cyberveilig Nederland
B.P.F. Jacobs, Radboud University Nijmegen
O. Janssen, AON
H. de Jong, National Police
T.H.J. Joustra, Dutch Safety Board
M. Jutte, Hudson Cybertec
E. Kamps, Crossyn Automotive BV
N. Kastelein, Ministry of Finance
S. Kewal, Ministry of the Interior and Kingdom Relations
R. Kleijmer, DNB (Central Bank of the Netherlands)
J. Knops, National Coordinator for Security and Counterterrorism
O. Koeroo, KPN
H.C.D. Korvinus, Ministry of General Affairs
M. Krom, PostNL (Netherlands Post Office)
L.W. van der Laan, D66 (Dutch political party)
A.C.A.P. van Lammeren, Netherlands Environmental Assessment Agency
M. Leenaars, NLnet Foundation
M.J. van Leeuwen, Association of Insurers
T. van Lieshout, Central West Brabant Safety Region
H.A.M. Luiijf, Luiijf Consultancy
N. Mallens, VNO-NCW
E. Medendorp, Dutch Safety Board
R. Miedema, City of Rotterdam
E.M.L. Moerel, Tilburg Law School
Molenaar, City of Rotterdam
E.R. Muller, Dutch Safety Board
A.A. Muntslag - Bakker, Cyber Security Council
T. Netelenbos, ECP, Platform for the Information Society
W.J.K. Nierstrasz, City of Rotterdam
Nieuwesteeg, Erasmus University Rotterdam
J.A. Nijhuis, Schiphol Group
D.G.M. O'Floinn, National Coordinator for Security and Counterterrorism
A.M. Ottolini, Evides Water Company
A.K.J. van Petersen, National Cyber Security Centre
S. van der Pijnse van der Aa, Dutch Safety Board
A.C. Pleyte, National Coordinator Groningen
M. Postma, Fox-IT
Quist, National Coordinator for Security and Counterterrorism
H.J. Reinders, DNB (Central Bank of the Netherlands)

S.J.G. Reyn, Ministry of Defence
S. Riedstra, Ministry of Justice and Security
G.N. Roes, Council of State
Y.C.M.T. van Rooy, Dutch Association of Hospitals
R. Roozendaal, Ministry of Health, Welfare and Sport
U. Rosenthal, Advisory Board for Science, Technology and Innovation
van Ruijven, Institute of Physical Safety (IFV)
T. van Ruijven, TNO
H. Schrijvers, SIM-CI/Alliander
B. Sluijter, National Coordinator for Security and Counterterrorism
F. Soeteman, Association of Insurers
J.W.E. Spies, Municipality of Alphen aan den Rijn
W.W. Stevens, Ministry of General Affairs
Stuurman, Tilburg University
Sybesma, Victim Support Fund
J.J. Sylvester, National Ombudsman
J. van Tol, Ministry of Economic Affairs and Climate
M. in 't Veld, National Coordinator Groningen
P.G. van der Velden, Centerdata
K. Verhoeven, D66 (Dutch political party)
A.C. Vervooren, City of Rotterdam
M.F. Verweij, Wageningen University & Research
F.W. Vijselaar, Ministry of Economic Affairs and Climate
P. van Vollenhoven, Society and Safety Foundation
G.H. de Vries, University of Amsterdam
H. de Vries, National Cyber Security Centre
R. de Vries, Port of Rotterdam
R.H. van Wanroij, National Coordinator for Security and Counterterrorism
R. Wenselaar, Menzis
Wielenga, Council for the Environment and Infrastructure
M. van Wieren, AON
G.W.P.J. Wismans, National Coordinator for Security and Counterterrorism
M. Zannoni, COT Institute for Security and Crisis Management
P.M. Zorko, National Coordinator for Security and Counterterrorism
R.F.B. van Zutphen, National Ombudsman
R. van Zwol, Council of State

Contents

Abbreviations

AIVD	Algemene Inlichtingen- en Veiligheidsdienst (General Intelligence and Security Service)
AMS-IX	Amsterdam Internet Exchange
BGP	Border Gateway Protocol
CERT	Computer Emergency Response Team
CERT-EU	Computer Emergency Response Team, European Union
CPB	Centraal Planbureau (Netherlands Bureau for Economic Policy Analysis)
CSIRT	Computer Security Incident Response Team
CSR	Cyber Security Raad (Cyber Security Council)
DDoS	Distributed Denial of Service
DNB	De Nederlandsche Bank (Central Bank of the Netherlands)
DNS	Domain Name System
DTC	Digital Trust Centre
DTM	Dynamic Traffic Management
EC3	European Cyber Crime Centre
EDA	European Defence Agency
ENISA	European Union Agency for Network and Information Security
EPSC	European Political Strategy Centre
FIRST	Forum of Incident Response and Security Teams
ICT	Information and Communication Technology
IMF	International Monetary Fund
IoT	Internet of Things
IP	Internet Protocol
IPCR	Integrated Political Crisis Response
IRB	ICT Response Board
ISAC	Information Sharing Analysis Centre
MIVD	Militaire Inlichtingen- en Veiligheidsdienst (Military Intelligence and Security Service)
NAFIN	Netherlands Armed Forces Integrated Network
NATO	North Atlantic Treaty Organization

NCCIC	National Cyber Security and Communications Integration Centre
NCSC	National Cyber Security Centre
NCTV	Nationaal Coördinator Terrorismebestrijding en Veiligheid (National Coordinator for Security and Counterterrorism)
NDN	Nationaal Detectie Netwerk (National Detection Network)
NHC	Nationaal Handboek Crisisbesluitvorming (National Guide for Crisis Decision-Making)
NHS	National Health Service
OECD	Organization for Economic Cooperation and Development
OM	Openbaar Ministerie (Netherlands Public Prosecution Service)
PBL	Planbureau voor de Leefomgeving (Netherlands Environmental Assessment Agency)
PKI	Public Key Infrastructure
RIVM	Rijksinstituut voor Volksgezondheid en Milieu (National Institute for Public Health and the Environment)
RLI	Raad voor de Leefomgeving en Infrastructuur (Council for the Environment and Infrastructure)
SIDN	Stichting Internet Domeinregistratie Nederland (Netherlands Foundation for Internet Domain Registration)
TIBER	Threat intelligence-based ethical red teaming
WODC	Wetenschappelijk Onderzoek en Documentatiecentrum (Scientific Research and Documentation Centre)
WRR	Wetenschappelijke Raad voor het Regeringsbeleid (Netherlands Scientific Council for Government Policy)

Chapter 1
Fighting Digital Fires

Suppose a 'fire' breaks out in the digital realm. Which fire brigade would we call?
Do we sufficiently understand the vulnerabilities? What should we prioritize in our
fire-fighting efforts? What powers do the authorities have to minimize the number of
victims and to limit the damage? Are their powers commensurate for our digital
world? These questions take on renewed urgency when the 'fire' in question is not
limited to the digital domain but, left unchecked, has the ability to disrupt the 'real
world' and undermine confidence in public institutions. Answering these questions
inevitably leads to fundamental questions about the role of government, citizens and
businesses. These themes are the subject of this report.

1.1   Incidents – Large and Small – Are a Fact of Life

Incidents involving our digital infrastructure are to be expected in our rapidly digitizing society.[1] Governments and other public and private organizations around the
world are warning us about the risks. Indeed, various types of disruption have
already occurred.[2] The problems can usually be resolved quickly, with the effects
limited to inconvenience – these are the minor blazes. But in recent years, we have
also witnessed incidents with much more serious consequences:

- In the Netherlands, the 2011 DigiNotar crisis was the first to reveal our dependence on digital technology.[3] Hackers released forged certificates from the certification authority, compromising the reliability of all DigiNotar certificates,
  which browser providers such as Microsoft threatened to declare invalid. This

---

[1] Section 1.2 discusses terms such as *incident, disruption, disaster, societal disruption* and *digital disruption* in more detail.

[2] Clarke & Knake, 2019 ; Schneier, 2018; Greenberg, 2018.

[3] Prins, 2011.

© The Author(s) 2021
E. Schrijvers et al., *Preparing for Digital Disruption*, Research for Policy,
https://doi.org/10.1007/978-3-030-77838-5_1

meant that important functions of government, such as customs clearance for goods and the payment of surcharges, could no longer be carried out. The incident was resolved but made headlines around the world by revealing the vulnerability and importance of private certification authorities for secure communication over the internet.[4]

- In 2016, a DDoS attack targeted the American company Dyn, a Domain Name System (DNS) provider.[5] Internet platforms such as Twitter, Netflix and Reddit could not be accessed in the United States and Europe for most of the day. The attack was carried out with the Mirai botnet, consisting of compromised consumer devices such as webcams and digital video recorders. DNS providers translate web addresses into IP numbers, enabling computers to access websites. Some described the attack on Dyn as an attack on the internet itself.[6]

- In 2017, *WannaCry* – which at the time was assumed to be ransomware but has since been attributed to North Korea – infected the computers of Chinese universities, Spanish electricity and gas companies, the French car company Renault and the rail transport company Deutsche Bahn, among others. The most prominent victim was the UK's National Health Service. The services of around 600 healthcare institutions were disrupted, including the cancellation of about 19,000 patient appointments; some accident and emergency locations were unable to provide care to patients and had to be relocated. It took the NHS about 1 week to return to normal. Estimated cost: £92 million.

- Also in 2017, hackers working for the Russian military distributed the *NotPetya* ransomware by exploiting vulnerabilities in Ukrainian accounting software, which they had previously hacked. The virus affected companies and organizations worldwide, with reports of damage running into the billions. The Rotterdam division of the Maersk container company fell victim to the cross-border chain of contamination. Like many other ports worldwide, container transport ground to a halt. So did the surrounding rail links and highways, causing congestion and long traffic jams. In the Dutch town of Oss, the production of medicines by the pharmaceutical company MSD came to a stop. MSD also lost a great deal of documentation.

- In March 2018, the US city of Atlanta fell victim to a digital attack. Months later, many basic municipal services were still unavailable. The city lost tens of millions of dollars; numerous data files, including police files, were lost for good.[7] Many other municipalities, corporations and public institutions such as universities have since fallen victim to similar ransomware attacks, often paying the attackers to restore their systems and retrieve lost information.

---

[4] Van der Meulen, 2013.

[5] https://en.wikipedia.org/wiki/2016_Dyn_cyberattack

[6] See WRR, 2015 for the importance of basic protocols such as DNS for the internet's functioning.

[7] https://nakedsecurity.sophos.com/2018/06/08/atlanta-ransomware-attack-destroyed-years-of-police-dashcam-video/

- Human error, broken servers, software issues and external factors such as cable breaks and power failures can also jeopardize the functioning of digital infrastructure. In June 2019, Google Cloud suffered outages due to regular maintenance work[8] and could no longer support one-third of its own traffic. In the event of disruption, Google prioritizes the data traffic which should remain available. But the slowdown also affected Google's own capacity to recover, which led to a longer outage than would otherwise have been the case. Like Amazon Web Services in 2017, Google Cloud had already suffered an outage in 2018 due to a simple typing error.[9] In all of these cases, the outages did not last for more than a few hours; it remains unclear whether large cloud providers could cope with longer outages. The effects of such disruptions will grow as more and more companies switch to cloud-based services and more societal processes come to depend on these providers.

The severity of these incidents continues to be debated. The global financial damage caused by *WannaCry* was enormous and human lives were endangered. The same was true of the *NotPetya* attack, the effects of which had similar cross-border patterns. But did these attacks truly disrupt society? Although the DigiNotar incident in the Netherlands revealed unforeseen problems, they were resolved. The record thus far has muddied efforts to place the threat of digital disruption on the political agenda and generally accept the seriousness and urgency of this problem. Nevertheless, we would be amiss to downplay the potential of such incidents or to imagine that a major disruption is unrealistic.

1.2   Disruptions at the Heart of Society

The potential scale of disruption has grown enormously in recent years. According to the OECD project 'Future Global Shocks' back in 2011, few cyber-related events had the potential to cause a global shock.[10] But the authors were already pointing to the growing risk of financial damage due to compromised computers and telecommunications services. They also added that digital services would be essential for recovery operations following other types of large-scale disasters.[11] Almost a decade later, both observations have been proven prescient. Crisis management and disaster

---

[8] See: https://www.wired.com/story/google-cloud-outage-catch-22/?CNDID=53898727&CNDID=53898727&bxid=Mjc0Mzg0ODIwMDk5S0&hasha=100c13df07dc1abb3dd77f24de416e4d&hashb=c00c411b0670ffa64b106b13483864092cbfb5d4&mbid=nl_060819_daily_list1_p4&source=DAILY_NEWSLETTER&utm_brand=wired&utm_mailing=WIRED%20NL%20060819%20 (1) & utm_medium = email & utm_source = en. For Google's own report on the outage see: https://status.cloud.google.com/incident/cloud-networking/19009

[9] See: https://www.geekwire.com/2017/amazon-explains-massive-aws-outage-says-employee-error-took-servers-offline-promises-changes/

[10] Sommer & Brown, 2011.

[11] Cf. Prins, 2010.

relief today are unthinkable without digital tools, the Covid-19 crisis being a case in point. And the potential impact of incidents involving digital infrastructure has only grown: in geographical scope as well as how they affect real-world infrastructure and the daily lives of citizens.

Digital disruptions can now jeopardize the core processes of society. *WannaCry* caused parts of the UK's healthcare system to fail; DigiNotar threatened to disrupt the Dutch government's digital services and parts of the payment system; the hack in Atlanta led to the loss of important public data. In the meantime, we have already moved into the next phase: the taking out of facilities. In 2016, hackers infected a power station in Kiev with malware, knocking out one-fifth of the capital's power-generating capacity[12] – an incident that will go down in history as the first time malicious actors managed to remotely switch off a public utility. Things have only accelerated since then. In 2017, hackers succeeded in gaining control of software in US power plants.[13] June 2019 saw media reports of disruptive malware that the US had placed in the Russian electricity grid.[14]

The costs for society are also rising. Lloyd's estimates the damage that would be caused by the failure of cloud services in the United States at 5 to 53 billion US dollars.[15] The IMF reports that the potential damage to financial institutions caused by cyber-attacks could run into the hundreds of billions of dollars. These are estimates; there have been too few incidents to calculate potential damage with any degree of certainty. Nor is there consensus over what losses different types of incidents could generate.[16] What is clear is that the potential for human victims and material damage is growing as society becomes ever more reliant on digital technologies. The US cyber expert Bruce Schneier explains:

> With smart homes, attacks can mean property damage. With banks, they can mean economic chaos. With power plants they can mean blackouts. With waste treatment plants they can mean toxic spills. With cars, planes and medical devices, they can mean death. With terrorists and nation-states, the security of entire economies and nations could be at stake.[17]

Digital attacks have become an instrument of geopolitical conflict as the traditional struggle for control over land, sea and airspace has been extended to the digital realm.[18] The struggle here is not about defining boundaries, but about sabotaging societal and economic processes and the strategic position of other countries. All in all, the question is no longer if – but *when* – we will need to deal with the consequences of a large-scale cyber-attack.

---

[12] Cf. Sanger, 2018, chapter 7.

[13] https://www.wired.com/story/hackers-gain-switch-flipping-access-to-us-power-systems/

[14] See https://www.google.nl/amp/s/www.nytimes.com/2019/06/15/us/politics/trump-cyber-russia-grid.amp.html and https://www.google.nl/amp/s/www.nytimes.com/2019/06/17/world/europe/russia-us-cyberwar-grid.amp.html

[15] Lloyd's & Cyence, 2017.

[16] OECD, 2017.

[17] Schneier, 2018: 16.

[18] WRR, 2017.

1.3   There Is No Such Thing as 100% Security – But Are We Sufficiently Prepared for Disruption?

The growing scale, distribution and impact of incidents are partly due to the rapid pace at which the world is embracing digital technology.[19] Digital technology is also becoming ever more complex with the exponential growth of data, computing power, and the exchange of data between devices, between people and devices, and between technology and the physical environment. We are now adding chips and sensors to almost everything, while everything is being connected to the internet. The next phase of this development – the 'Internet of Things' and artificial intelligence – will make all kinds of processes even faster and smarter. The result is that interaction between the digital world and the physical world is becoming ever more intense. In some sectors, the digital realm and the physical realm are already difficult to distinguish.

Alongside countries like Denmark, Estonia, Singapore, Finland, the US, Norway, the UK and Sweden, the Netherlands is at the forefront of the digital evolution. It has high connectivity, a digitally adept population, and highly digitized public services. Actively supported by the government, consumers and companies are embracing all kinds of digital activities. But every technological development has its flip side: advantages (the 'highway to efficiency') as well as disadvantages (the 'highway to failure').[20] Digitization is no exception.[21] Digitization creates prosperity, individual freedom and convenience; countless nations are fully committed to these aspirations. But digitization also brings new vulnerabilities and dependencies,[22] to the economy and core societal processes as well as to the safety of people and their property.[23] Although the stakes are presumably higher for highly digitized countries, countries lower on international indexes of digitization are not immune.

Many governments are well aware of society's growing vulnerability to digital disruption.[24] The UK government expects that the country, measures notwithstanding, will suffer a major cyber-attack.[25] In Austria, there is discussion of a 'Digitalen

---

[19] Schwab, 2016.

[20] Turner, 1978; Perrow, 1983; Boin, 2017.

[21] Pupillo, 2018: 1.

[22] Schneier, 2018; World Economic Forum, 2017: 6; NCTV, 2018a, b: 5.

[23] Internet Society, 2017: 10.

[24] There has been no systematic international comparison of cyber security policies and institutions. See Van der Zwan and Spit (2015) for a cursory comparison of efforts to protect vital infrastructure; Janczewski and Caelli (2016) for the position of some smaller countries in cyber-attacks; Boeke (2016) for the role of the defence ministry in cyber-attacks in Denmark, the Netherlands, Estonia and the Czech Republic.

[25] For the British cyber strategy see: https://assets.publishing.service.gov.uk/government/uploads/system/uploads/attachment_data/file/567242/national_cyber_security_strategy_2016.pdf

For parliamentary deliberations and reports: https://publications.parliament.uk/pa/jt201719/jtselect/jtnatsec/1708/1708.pdf

Stillstand' scenario caused by cascade effects.[26] The United States and France have developed systems of categorization for cyber incidents to determine the appropriate time to take direct action. The European Union has various initiatives to ensure that digital disruption can be adequately addressed.[27]

All of these cyber-security measures aim to *prevent* major incidents. But there is no such thing as total information security – an inconvenient truth that is often forgotten. Whether inside or outside the digital domain, incidents can and will occur, leading to real-world disruption. Countries have contingency plans as well as legislation and regulation to deal with major disruptions due to natural and industrial disasters. But when it comes to cyber security, contingency planning has been much more limited. While many policy documents include sections on the possibility of serious disruption, their primary focus is achieving a higher level of protection or measures to reduce risks.[28] The scenario of major disruption thus serves to encourage people to take prevention more seriously. Only rarely are concrete measures set out for dealing with the consequences of incidents that do occur.[29]

1.4   Structure of This Report

Cyber security and the prevention of digital disruption are not the focus of this report. We begin with the premise that we must face the real possibility of a scenario in which digital disruption leads to societal disruption. In short, we have to think about our response in concrete terms.[30] This report thus inquires: *How can government better prepare itself for societal disruption in a digitizing society?*

The report is structured as follows. Section 2 defines societal disruption to clarify the type of events we are addressing. Section 3 analyses how digitization is changing the context in which these events occur. Section 4 discusses the challenges that the government faces in terms of preparedness, detection, combating, and

---

[26] http://www.darc-c12.de/system/files/Projektbericht-Digitaler-Stillstand-final.pdf

[27] For example: http://ec.europa.eu/transparency/regdoc/rep/3/2017/NL/C-2017-6100-F1-NL-MAIN-PART-1.PDF and http://ec.europa.eu/transparency/regdoc/rep/3/2017/NL/C-2017-6100-F1-NL-ANNEX-1-PART-1.PDF

[28] Cyber security is defined in Dutch policy as 'the entirety of measures to prevent damage due to the disruption, failure or misuse of information and communication technology and, where damage does occur, to rectify this'.

[29] An example is the letter from the Dutch State Secretary of the Interior and Kingdom Relations addressing information security in government. It states that 'Citizens, businesspeople and other organizations must be able to continue to rely on the government, including in the digital age' (Ministry of the Interior & Kingdom Relations, 2018: 6). Measures include 'ensuring that important digital facilities of government are sufficiently able to withstand failure or outage.' But except for the capacity to generally communicate about responses to incidents, the measures do not concern responding to incidents once they have happened.

[30] Cf. Prins, 2017.

recovering from major digital incidents. Section 5 presents our conclusions and recommendations.

We conclude that digitization has led to new forms of societal disruption and thus to a new set of tasks for government. Our recommendations concern policies regarding dependencies, critical infrastructure, competencies, priorities in combating the consequences of incidents, and compensation for victims, including the insurability of damages

References

Boeke, S. (2016). *First responder or last resort? The role of the ministry of defence in national cyber crisis management in four European countries.* Leiden University.

Boin, R. A. (2017). *De grenzeloze crisis: Uitdagingen voor politiek en bestuur* [Crisis without borders: Challenges for politics and management]. Inaugural lecture, Leiden University.

Clarke, R.A. & Knake R.K. (2019). The fifth domain. Defending our country, our companies, and ourselves in the age of cyber threats. Penguin Press.

Greenberg, A. (2018). *The untold story of NotPetya, the most devastating cyberattack in history.* https://www.wired.com/story/notpetya-cyberattack-ukraine-russia-code-crashed-the-world/

Internet Society. (2017). *Global internet report 2017. Paths to our digital future.* https://future.internetsociety.org/2017/wp-content/uploads/sites/3/2017/09/2017-Internet-Society-Global-Internet-Report-Paths-to-Our-Digital-Future.pdf

Janczewski, J., & Caelli, W. (Eds.). (2016). *Cyber conflicts and small states.* Ashgate.

Lloyd's and Cyence. (2017). *Counting the cost: Cyber exposure decoded.* Lloyd's.

Ministry of the Interior and Kingdom Relations. (2018, October 16). *Brief inzake verhogen informatieveiligheid bij de overheid* [Letter on increasing information security in the government]. Ministry of the Interior and Kingdom Relations.

NCTV. (2018a). *Cybersecuritybeeld Nederland 2018* [Cyber security assessment Netherlands 2018]. NCTV.

NCTV. (2018b). *Nationale veiligheid bij overnames en investeringen of inkoop en aanbesteding* [National security in take-overs and investments or service provision and tenders]. NCTV. https://www.nctv.nl/binaries/WEB_113154_NCTV_Veiligheid_bij_overnames_tcm31-334520.pdf

OECD. (2017). *Enhancing the role of insurance in cyber risk management.* OECD.

Perrow, C. (1983). The organizational context of human factors engineering. *Administrative Science Quarterly, 28*(4), 521–541.

Prins, J. E. J. (2010). Digital tools: risks and opportunities for victims: Explorations in e-victimology. In J. van Dijk & R. Letschert (Eds.), *The new faces of victimhood. Studies in global justice.* Springer.

Prins, J. E. J. (2011). Een hack bij DigiNotar [A hack at DigiNotar]. *Nederlands Juristenblad, 86*(30), 1585.

Prins, J. E. J. (2017). Schadelijke beestjes [Damaging bugs]. *Nederlands Juristenblad, 92*(8), 507.

Pupillo, L. (2018). EU cybersecurity and the paradox of progress. *CEPS Policy Insights 2018/06.*

Sanger, D. A. (2018). *The perfect weapon: War, sabotage and fear in the cyber age.* Crown.

Schneier, B. (2018). *Click here to kill everybody: Security and survival in a hyper-connected world.* W.W. Norton & Company.

Schwab, K. (2016). *The fourth industrial revolution.* Crown.

Sommer, P., & Brown, I. (2011). *Reducing systemic cybersecurity risk.* OECD.

Turner, B. A. (1978). *Man-made disasters.* Wykeham.

Van der Meulen, N. (2013). DigiNotar: Dissecting the first Dutch digital disaster. *Journal of Strategic Security, 6*(2), 44–58.

Van der Zwan, E., & Spit, M. (2015). De internationale stand van zaken in de bescherming van vitale infrastructuur [The international state of affairs in protecting vital infrastructure]. *Magazine Nationale Veiligheid en Crisisbeheersing, 3*, 32–33.

World Economic Forum. (2017). *The global risks report 2017*. https://www.weforum.org/reports/the-global-risks-report-2017

WRR [Netherlands Scientific Council for Government Policy]. (2015). *De publieke kern van het internet. Naar een buitenlands internetbeleid* [The public core of the internet. Towards a foreign internet policy]. Amsterdam University Press. https://www.wrr.nl/publicaties/rapporten/2015/03/31/de-publieke-kern-van-het-internet

WRR [Netherlands Scientific Council for Government Policy]. (2017). *Veiligheid in een wereld van verbindingen* [Security in a connected world]. WRR. https://www.wrr.nl/publicaties/rapporten/2017/05/10/veiligheid-in-een-wereld-van-verbindingen

Chapter 2
Societal Disruption

2.1 Introduction

This section first explains the concept of 'societal disruption' to clarify what type of events we are addressing in this report. If events have a significant digital component, we speak of 'digital disruption'. Because societal disruption in policy practice is often linked to national security and 'critical assets', we also consider the classification of critical processes and critical infrastructure.

2.2 Societal Disruption

As societal disruption follows catastrophic events such as major floods or pandemics like Covid-19, it is intricately linked to the concept of risk. Risk is often defined in the literature as 'probability x consequence'.[1] Societal disruption concerns the consequences of that risk: the risk that damage will actually occur. While policy documents often refer to 'societal disruption', there is no clear definition of the term. Clearly, a major disaster would disrupt society. But it is more difficult to define a clear threshold as different types of events will differentially disrupt society, the market and government. Nor does disruption have to start at a clearly defined point. Like a smouldering peat fire, disruption may begin under the surface, its full extent only becoming apparent later. We explain the meaning and scope of the concept of societal disruption below by discussing: (1) 'normal' societal functioning; (2) the severity of disruption; (3) the role of perception; and (4) the duration of disruption.

---

[1] See WRR, 2008: 53–86 for an explanation of the 'classical' approach to risk.

© The Author(s) 2021
E. Schrijvers et al., *Preparing for Digital Disruption*, Research for Policy,
https://doi.org/10.1007/978-3-030-77838-5_2

2.2.1   A Disruption of Everyday Life

Societal disruption implies the disruption of everyday societal processes. By 'everyday societal processes', we mean the regular functioning of the institutions of government, society and the market. If everyday societal processes can no longer
function adequately – whether due to additional costs or inadequate public confidence – this counts as serious disruption, with consequences for society, economy
and government, including justice, elections and the legislative process. We discuss
the 'normal functioning' of society's institutions both in terms of verifiable damage
to the continuity of society and people's perceptions of disruption.[2]

2.2.2   'Serious' Disruption: Failure of Core Processes

In the event of serious disruption, societal processes such as payments, the internet,
public transport, healthcare, drinking water and electricity may stop functioning or
switch to a less efficient mode. The continuity of society would no longer be guaranteed. Long traffic jams or queues could form, large quantities of goods could pile
up, information and services could become inaccessible or unreliable, so that many
everyday activities would no longer be possible. At this point, disruption would also
lead to major economic damage. It may be direct damage, such as to flood defences,
homes, computers and company installations, but also indirect damage due to business failures or the disruption of the activities of third parties. Finally, there may be
physical casualties: human injuries and deaths.

2.2.3   Perceived Disruption

All of this can, in principle, be verified and quantified, and expressed in financial
terms for compensation purposes, for instance. But alongside the material effects,
there is also the risk that citizens lose confidence in the institutions of government,
the market economy, or the society in which they live. Would they experience the
disruption as an inconvenience or as a serious violation of their daily lives? The
answer depends on people's value systems[3] as well as the extent of their self-
reliance[4] during and after the disruption.

How people perceive the competence of private and public organizations, particularly that of the government, matters greatly. Did the government take adequate
preventive measures? Was it able to take swift action to restore the normal

---

[2] Cf. PBL, 2014: 7–11.

[3] Douglas & Wildavski, 1982; Hood, 1998.

[4] Cf. WRR, 2017b.

functioning of society? If citizens, companies or organizations feel they can no longer rely on the continuity of normal societal functions, the foundations of the democratic constitutional state may be undermined. What makes digitization particularly problematic is the blurring of geographical boundaries; it may not always be in the power of national governments to quickly restore the normal functioning of society.[5]

The rule of law – which provides fundamental certainty in our society – is based on the premise that we live in a nation-state that can legitimately exercise a monopoly of violence within a clearly defined territory. If this principle is undermined, for example because the state can no longer successfully claim this monopoly, people may lose faith in society and the rule of law. In the event of serious digital disruption, it would also be unclear which resources the state can call on.[6] Such considerations would inevitably exacerbate the public perception of disruption.

Whether we are talking about an interruption to social services, economic damage, the number of victims, or the loss of confidence in society and government, these must reach a certain scale to merit the use of the term 'societal disruption'.

2.2.4   Duration of Disruption

A gradual, possibly unnoticed series of minor disruptions may have the same cumulative effect as an event that explodes onto our consciousness. In the former, the consequences of an event remain under the radar and only become clear gradually. The steady spread of disinformation, for example, undermines public confidence in institutions, which can harm the functioning of society over the long term. In the latter, cause and effect are largely indistinguishable; the seriousness of the situation is immediately obvious.

The passage of time is an important factor in the costs of disruption. Longer disruptions mean higher costs.[7] Ultimately, the adverse consequences of an event and assessments of damage will unfold over time.[8] More broadly, this also applies to the reputation of companies, organizations and governments. Inadequate detection systems and sluggish responses will impact the public's confidence in government, which by definition is expected to respond to serious situations swiftly and effectively.

---

[5] Bovens, 1998; WRR, 1998.

[6] Digitization poses anew what constitutes violence; it no longer only involves physical violence, but also new forms of 'digital violence'.

[7] Jocqué, 2016. For the costs of 'cyber breaches' relative to time of detection, see e.g. EPSC, 2017: 4.

[8] Lindenbergh & Hebly, 2016.

2.3   Critical Infrastructure and Critical Processes

Governments often view societal disruption through the lenses of national security and critical infrastructure. For the Dutch government, national security encompasses various 'critical' interests: territorial integrity, economic security, ecological security, physical security and social and political stability. The definition of national security has recently been extended to include 'other situations that (may) have a major impact on society'.[9] These include 'critical' processes that are so crucial that their failure or disruption would lead to immediate societal disruption or undermine national security. Together, these processes form the Netherlands' 'critical infrastructure'.[10]

Critical infrastructure denotes a range of services upon which society depends. Critical infrastructure must be protected from natural and technological disasters (e.g. floods and nuclear accidents). More recent understandings of critical infrastructure, however, transcend the traditional focus on national defence and military considerations. The focus of security policy has expanded beyond hostile actors, their capacity and motivations, to include the general vulnerabilities of society as a whole. Underlying this broader definition is the more diffuse spectrum of threats since the end of the Cold War, and new societal vulnerabilities due to our dependence on information systems.[11]

2.3.1   Critical Processes

The broader definition of critical infrastructure has led to a different approach to risk. In the absence of reliable data on the likelihood and impact of the risks society now faces, the focus has shifted from the potential causes to the potential consequences of the failure of processes critical to society's functioning. A classification of critical processes provides guidance for politicians, policymakers and other stakeholders to determine whether a particular situation should be considered serious – and thus whether the government should take action and, if so, how. After all, it is impossible to protect all societal functions against every possible threat all of the time, and we need to distinguish critical from non-critical processes. Assessments by the Dutch government have quantified the consequences of failure of each process as it bears on potential economic, physical and social harm. Consideration of

---

[9] NCTV, 2016: 8. These include 'a local or regional incident or accident with many casualties, an incident or accident abroad with a large number of Dutch casualties, or international events which affect the Netherlands'.

[10] See Parliamentary Papers II 2014/15, 30 821, no. 23 and Parliamentary Papers II 2015/16, 30 821, no. 32.

[11] Dunn Cavalty, 2007: 16; WRR, 2017a; Nationale Veiligheid Strategie 2019. [National Security Strategy 2019].

cascade effects resulted in two categories of critical processes, based on the seriousness of the impact of their failure.

The 'critical' nature of societal processes also depends on their organization and
the risk of disruption.[12] This includes the presence of back-up options and recovery
time – decisive factors for the extent of damage or the number of victims if things
go wrong. Impact is not a fixed measure; it depends on the resilience of the actors
responsible for the critical process in question.

Overviews of critical processes therefore differ, both over time and from country
to country. Governments compile different lists or add new areas to reflect the latest
threats. In 2017, the United States reclassified elections infrastructure as critical.[13]
Germany includes the media and certain cultural goods.[14] While healthcare regularly features in international overviews of critical infrastructure, Dutch hospitals
and other healthcare institutions have recently been dropped from the list.[15] As in
the DigiNotar case, the critical importance of certain processes often only becomes
clear after they suffer disruption. We will return to the implications of these national
differences in the next section.

2.4   Digital Disruption

Digitization means that societal functions and processes are vulnerable in new and
unexpected ways. This vulnerability applies to both regular processes and processes
classified as critical by the government, since most critical processes are already
bound up with digital infrastructure. By 'digital infrastructure', we mean all facilities for the storage, exchange and processing of digital data. Until about 10 years
ago, the risk of the disruption or failure of these facilities was absent from almost all
national and international risk analyses. This has changed over the past decade. The
risk of the disruption or failure of digital infrastructure has risen rapidly through the
ranking of risks that would have disruptive consequences for society.[16]

The disruption or failure of digital infrastructure can have many causes, from
accidental (errors) or deliberate human actions (often of a criminal or at least unlawful nature) to the spontaneous failure of systems or the semi-autonomous behaviour
of machines. There are also more indirect causes such as fires, power failures or
floods that damage servers. These causes can occur separately or in combination
and can result in both acute and gradual disruption. Where societal disruption has an
important digital component, we refer to 'digital disruption'.

---

[12] Sharma, 2017: 33–36.

[13] https://fas.org/sgp/crs/misc/IF10677.pdf

[14] https://www.bmi.bund.de/SharedDocs/downloads/DE/publikationen/themen/bevoelkerungss-
chutz/kritis.pdf?__blob=publicationFile&v=3

[15] https://zoek.officielebekendmakingen.nl/kst-27529-158.html

[16] The World Economic Forum scores the same risks each year, giving us an idea of how digital
disruptions rank relative to other risks.

The scope of this report does not extend to the exact likelihood and consequences of digital disruption. Recent studies have already addressed these questions, both in the Netherlands[17] and abroad.[18] The potential of digital disruption leading to significant economic damage and social unrest is real, and is the premise of our analysis in the following sections. Our aim is to formulate an agenda for measures that could be taken to prepare society for such disruption, focusing specifically on what government can do.

2.5 Conclusion

We use the term 'societal disruption' to refer to serious disruptions to the regular functioning of society. What constitutes 'regular' societal functioning and 'serious' disruption will depend not only on the interruption of core processes in society but on the confidence that citizens, companies and public and private organizations have in them. The two feed into one another: a major disruptive event will inevitably undermine public confidence in society as well. At the same time, a series of smaller events may exacerbate the sense of threat and undermine confidence in the government, even if the event's actual significance is limited.

By identifying critical processes, the government seeks to set priorities and ensure that not all disruptions are classified as 'major'. This helps to direct scarce resources to where they can be used most effectively and legitimately. The list of critical processes is the result of an assessment of their importance and vulnerability to disruption and failure. That the disruption and failure of digital infrastructure can also have socially disruptive effects is now widely recognized. In the following sections, we use the concept of digital disruption to describe these effects.

References

ANV (Analistennetwerk Nationale Veiligheid) [National Security Analysts Network]. (2018). *Horizonscan Nationale Veiligheid 2018*. https://www.thehaguesecuritydelta.com/media/com_hsd/report/216/document/ANV-Horizonscan-Nationale-Veiligheid-2018.pdf

Bovens, M. A. P. (1998). *De digitale rechtstaat. Beschouwingen over informatiemaatschappij en rechtstaat* [The digital nation state. Reflections on the information society and the rule of law]. Samsom.

DeNardis, L. (2014). *The global war for internet governance*. Yale University Press.

Douglas, M. & Wildavski, A. (1982). *Risk and culture*. University of California Press.

---

[17] E.g. ANV, 2018: 22.

[18] E.g. World Economic Forum, 2017; Sommer & Brown, 2011; Lloyd's & Cyence, 2017. For the relationship between cyber security governance and national security, see DeNardis, 2014: 86, 104–106.

Dunn Cavalty, M. (2007). Critical information infrastructure: Vulnerabilities, threats and responses. *ICTs and International Security, 3*. https://www.peacepalacelibrary.nl/ebooks/files/UNIDIR_pdf-art2643.pdf

EPSC [European Political Strategy Centre]. (2017). *Building an effective European cyber shield. Taking EU cooperation to the next level* https://ec.europe.eu/epsc/publications/strategic-notes/building-effective-european-cyber-shield_en#-1

Hood, C. (1998). *The art of the state. Culture, rhetoric and public management.* Oxford University Press.

Jocqué, G. (2016, 2016). Tijdsverloop en schadevergoeding [Damage compensation over time]. *Tijdschrijft voor Privaatrecht*, (4), 1375–1434.

Lindenbergh, S. D., & Hebly, M. R. (2016). Schadebegroting en tijdsverloop. In *Preadviezen 2016* (pp. 301–361) http://hdl.handle.net/1765/95657

Lloyd's and Cyence. (2017). *Counting the cost: Cyber exposure decoded.* Lloyd's.

Ministerie van Justitie en Veiligheid [Ministry of Justice and Security]. (2019). *Strategie nationale veiligheid* [Strategy national security]. https://www.rijksoverheid.nl/documenten/rapporten/2019/06/07/tk-bijlage-nationale-strategie-2019

NCTV [National Coordinator for Security and Counterterrorism]. (2016). *Nationaal handboek crisisbesluitvorming* [National handbook for crisis decision making]. NCTV.

PBL (Netherlands Environmental Assessment Agency). (2014). *Maatschappelijke ontwrichting en overstromingen* [Societal disruption and flooding]. PBL.

Sharma, M. (2017). *Securing critical information infrastructure: Global perspectives and practices.* Institute for Defence Studies and Analyses. https://idsa.in/system/files/monograph/monograph60.pdf

Sommer, P., & Brown, I. (2011). *Reducing systemic cybersecurity risk.* OECD.

World Economic Forum. (2017). *The global risks report 2017.* https://www.weforum.org/reports/the-global-risks-report-2017

WRR [Netherlands Scientific Council for Government Policy]. (1998). *Staat zonder land: een verkenning van bestuurlijke gevolgen van informatie- en communicatietechnologie* [State without a nation: an exploration of the administrative consequences of Information and Communication Technology]. Sdu Uitgevers. https://www.wrr.nl/publicaties/rapporten/1998/03/09/staat-zonder-land-een-verkenning-van-bestuurlijke-gevolgen-van-informatie--en-communicatietechnologie

WRR [Netherlands Scientific Council for Government Policy]. (2008). *Onzekere veiligheid. Verantwoordelijkheden rond fysieke veiligheid* [Uncertain security. Responsibilities for physical safety]. Amsterdam University Press. https://www.wrr.nl/publicaties/rapporten/2008/10/01/onzekere-veiligheid

WRR [Netherlands Scientific Council for Government Policy]. (2017a). *Veiligheid in een wereld van verbindingen* [Security in a connected world]. WRR. https://www.wrr.nl/publicaties/rapporten/2017/05/10/veiligheid-in-een-wereld-van-verbindingen

WRR [Netherlands Scientific Council for Government Policy]. (2017b). *Weten is nog geen doen. Een realistisch perspectief op zelfredzaamheid* [Knowledge is not the same as action. A realistic perspective on self-reliance]. WRR. https://www.wrr.nl/publicaties/rapporten/2017/04/24/weten-is-nog-geen-doen

Chapter 3
Digitization and Societal Disruption

3.1 Introduction

Digitization is placing new demands on how we deal with incidents that threaten to undermine core societal functions and processes. Societal disruption will almost inevitably flow from the disruption or failure of digital infrastructure given the interdependence of the digital and physical realms. Digitization also poses new challenges for policy makers as the use of digital technology leads to complex, cross-border networks with geopolitical implications.

3.2 Our Growing Dependence on Digital Technology

The role of digital technology in society has exploded in recent decades with the growth of 'datafication', computing power and connectivity. While each trend brings countless new opportunities to society, they have also altered the risk landscape for citizens, companies, organizations and states.

3.2.1 Datafication

Ever more societal processes are based on the flow of data and information.[1] 'Datafication' has three main features.[2] The exponential growth of data being stored and exchanged is due not only to targeted collection and voluntary provision, but

---

[1] WRR, 2011a.
[2] WRR, 2015: 27–28.

© The Author(s) 2021
E. Schrijvers et al., *Preparing for Digital Disruption*, Research for Policy,
https://doi.org/10.1007/978-3-030-77838-5_3

also to constant production through automated processes.[3] Data is also coming to play a more autonomous role in the functioning of society, with datafication changing the nature of data collection and its analysis through algorithms. The growing range of applications means that for ever more sectors and for ever more people, data is the raw material on which 'real-world' processes are based and 'real-world' actions are taken. Data has thus become an essential factor of production for countless companies. Public services rely on data, for example the interwoven system of healthcare and rent allowances.[4] For citizens, data is the oxygen that allows them to participate fully in society.

Datafication makes us more vulnerable to societal disruption by increasing the importance and vulnerability of data processes and files. A large number of recent incidents have shown user data to be inadequately secured, stolen by criminals, or held 'geopolitical hostage'. The scaling up of data-use not only exacerbates these vulnerabilities, but also means that ever more people can be affected. Some incidents have compromised the data of many millions of people. Malicious actors are also becoming more focused, seeking to hack into organizations such as banks and hospitals. With both the growing application of data and our dependence on it, problems involving the reliability, availability and integrity of data can also have more serious consequences, partly because they support core processes in everyday life. The failure or disruption of a digital system means that an important factor of production is no longer available or can no longer be relied on. It would be akin to dealing with a factory or a government department with no staff, or at least with a great many absent employees.

3.2.2 Computing Power

Increased computing power allows us to automate ever more complex processes. The most recent phase in this development is the use of algorithms, which allows us to process larger amounts of data than ever before and make decisions more rapidly as they are partly automated. When smart digital systems are properly programmed and trained, they are more reliable than humans in making rapid and complex decisions. But the speed and scale at which digitized systems make complex decisions means that things can quickly get out of hand when things go awry. Due to system complexity, problems can no longer be attributed to individuals, especially when multiple systems are communicating automatically. An illustrative incident is the Dow Jones Newswire's accidental publication of a report about Google's purchase of Apple in 2017, meant as a technical test. Automated trading robots responded within milliseconds, and the impact on stock prices was severe.[5] Another example

---

[3] Kitchin, 2014: 87–98.

[4] WRR, 2011a.

[5] https://www.nytimes.com/2017/10/10/business/media/dow-jones-google-apple.html

was the 2010 'flash crisis', when a trillion dollars in stock value evaporated in minutes due to unintended machine-to-machine interactions.[6] A more recent issue is the Russian interference in US elections, cunningly using automatic newsfeed systems, the scale of which only became apparent after extensive research.[7]

The failure of an automated system can result in societal functions and processes running less efficiently, becoming unsafe, or failing altogether.[8] An example is the 21 August 2018 rail outage at Schiphol Airport, caused by an error in the Dynamic Traffic Management System (DVM) software.[9] DVM software, used to manage the rail infrastructure around Schiphol, normally ensures that rail traffic routed through the Schiphol tunnel keeps flowing as smoothly as possible. When the DVM failed, the train routes between Amsterdam and Schiphol had to be managed manually. Instead of the normal average of 20 trains per hour, only 4 trains were able to run on this route for an extended period, affecting around 50,000 passengers. The incident revealed the importance of a well-functioning fall-back option and the availability of people with the skills to take control without the help of automated systems.

3.2.3 Connectivity

A third aspect of digitization is growing connectivity. The number of internet users continues to grow rapidly, as do the number of devices connected to the internet, the amount of data exchanged, and the number of applications and services managed online. Cloud computing, the Internet of Things (IoT) and artificial intelligence are expected to further reinforce connectivity, increasing the potential for serious consequences when societal disruption occurs. This is because efficient networks are crucial for the continuity of core societal processes and for quick and effective resolution if things go wrong.

For most digital services and applications, organizations can choose between different providers. But for some basic functions of the internet, there is no alternative.[10] Opinions vary regarding the vulnerability of the internet.[11] To date, the internet has been surprisingly resilient, finding its way around problems through its decentralized design. It is probably partly for this reason that no major crisis has yet occurred. The more connected an organization, network, or country, the better able it is to absorb shocks. At the same time, existing methods of attack may be scaled up – a DDoS attack using IoT devices, for instance.[12] Our growing reliance on the internet also means that greater connectivity can have further-reaching impact.

---

[6] Schneier, 2018: 85.

[7] Sanger (2018, 185, 255) mentions 80,000 posts on Facebook, possibly seen by 126 million people, and 288 million readers of Twitter messages. The impact of this remains unknown.

[8] See e.g. Stratix (2017: 4) for telecom failures.

[9] Van Gompel, 2018.

[10] WRR, 2015: 66.

[11] E.g. Van Eeten & Bauer, 2012; Van Ruijven & Duijnhoven, 2018.

[12] See e.g. Pras, 2014.

It is also difficult to determine which parts of the internet are truly indispensable.[13] While we can make technical distinctions, in practice this is not always useful. If large data centres, internet exchanges or authentication services fail, a large section of the population would suffer the consequences. The same applies to large cloud providers, as recent disruptions at Google and Amazon have shown. Technically, such problems would not affect the 'core' functions of the internet but would jeopardize many online services. The same applies to local physical infrastructure that links organizations to the internet or connects them in other ways, such as through mobile facilities.[14] Examples here include major network operators. Were one of these operators to go down due to for instance a power failure, this would not 'bring down the internet' but would restrict local connectivity and lead to major problems. Such organizations might in fact be 'too connected to fail'.[15]

3.3   Chains, Networks and Complexity Transcending Borders

The developments described above have led to major changes in how society is organized. Organizational processes have become intertwined with data systems, with the resulting chains and networks transcending national borders and growing in complexity. This makes it increasingly difficult to anticipate and respond to societal disruption.

3.3.1   Chains and Networks[16]

The availability of fast and cheap hardware and software has led organizations to base their production and services on real-time planning. This reduces storage costs, ensures the efficient use of capital and allows rapidly adapting to changed circumstances. But in the event of hardware failure or a network connection outage, the supply of goods can quickly dry up. The opposite happens at the other end of the chain, or elsewhere in the network, where goods may accumulate. *NotPetya* led to congestion at Maersk terminals around the world because the international registration system for containers ceased to function. With such flows and production chains interrupted, the economic security of the Netherlands would quickly enter the danger zone.[17]

---

[13] Broeders, 2017. See Mueller, 2017 for an explanation of fragmentation and the internet.

[14] Van Ruijven & Duijnhoven, 2018.

[15] Snyder, 2017.

[16] For the distinction between chains and networks, see WRR (2011a: 72). A 'chain' is a linear process in which different organizations work towards a shared end result outside their own organization. 'Network' refers to a relatively open relationship in which nodes are related to other nodes through multiple, traversing and often redundant connections.

[17] See WRR, 2017 for an analysis of flow security and how it is addressed in policy.

The internet and other large-scale networks allow controlling processes remotely. Organizations are increasingly making use of open networks, with devices communicating via protocols. This communication regularly takes place over the public internet to save on the costs of setting up a dedicated communication network. One problem with linking management systems to larger networks or to the internet is that these systems are sometimes outdated and no longer receive support from external suppliers or their own organization. While these systems may function safely in isolation, when linked to larger networks their vulnerability is a major risk as outsiders can access them much more easily. This applies to the systems used for drinking water, payment transactions, and the operation of canal locks and sluice gates.[18]

Chains and networks have intrinsic vulnerabilities and suffer disruption when their individual links fail. Information is scattered between actors, whose actions can unintentionally affect others in the chain. Digitization adds new vulnerabilities involving interfaces with the outside world, for example electronic patient records in hospitals and shared IT services such as data storage and cloud services.[19] Such applications add new parties to the system, creating new dependencies. They often also lead to more interactions, with all the accompanying risks of disruption.

Failures within chains and networks can result in cascade effects, particularly where components are intricately connected. Cascade effects occur when an ostensibly isolated problem affects the rest of the network, and possibly beyond it.[20] The consequences are far-reaching when many parties depend on the same service or supplier. This has traditionally been the case for the electricity supply, meaning that power outages top lists of events with major disruptive potential. The question today is whether parts of our digital infrastructure now occupy a similar position. Although hard evidence is hard to come by, a large-scale analysis of incidents in Europe shows that telecoms (37%) and internet (7%) services are second and third behind the energy sector (47%) when it comes to cascade effects.[21] Examples of major dependencies are legion, ranging from the use of Microsoft operating systems and Intel chips in most computers to banks and companies relying on the services of a handful of major international cyber-security companies.[22] The market for cloud services is also dominated by an extremely small number of companies (Amazon, Google, Microsoft and Salesforce).

---

[18] CPB, 2018: 14; Netherlands Court of Audit, 2019.

[19] Van Ruijven & Keijser, 2017; cf. Luiijf & Klaver, 2015; ENISA, 2018b.

[20] Klaver et al., 2013.

[21] Van Eeten et al., 2011.

[22] ChipSoft is now the largest supplier of new hospital electronic health records in the Netherlands, followed by Epic. Nine of the last ten implementations came from one of these two companies. https://www.zorgvisie.nl/hoe-konden-chipsoft-en-epic-zo-dominant-worden/

3.3.2 Beyond National Boundaries

Digitization means that almost every organization is vulnerable to disruptions in networks or supply chains because they depend on the products and services of third parties. At the same time, these networks and chains often cross national borders. Global connectivity, global production chains and IT facilities mean that the causes of a societally disruptive failure in one country can reach far beyond its borders. The internet itself is virtually without borders, meaning that any organization connected to the internet could, in principle, be attacked from anywhere in the world.[23] Due to these factors, societal disruption could quickly become borderless.[24]

The disappearance of national borders also manifests in how facilities and services are globally connected. Dutch companies, government institutions and citizens depend on a limited number of large – mainly US-based – software providers, IT service providers and security companies. Many cloud services simply run *somewhere* on the internet, not necessarily in one location. The use of cloud services may protect the continuity of processes, precisely because data is stored in multiple locations. Due to their elastic capacity, cloud providers are also better able to mitigate DDoS attacks and to update software as soon as patches become available. The revenue model of cloud providers also provides them with strong incentives to ensure the security of their facilities, which is often better than that of their customers.[25]

At the same time, the use of cloud services is creating new vulnerabilities. Cloud servers increase the number of parties, devices and applications involved, giving attackers more opportunities to access targeted systems. More data flows back and forth, increasing the chances of disruption. There are also concerns about delegating control over data and applications to cloud providers. Many cloud services consist of a layered and complex combination of platforms and services, involving contractors and subcontractors; this makes it unclear who is responsible for what – especially when things go wrong.[26] It is their size and the very large number of companies and organizations that use cloud providers that make them 'too big to fail'. At the same time, this makes them attractive geopolitical targets.

3.3.3 Complexity

The number of connections, products, services and actors means that systems are becoming increasingly complex and difficult to understand or quickly bring under control. Physical and digital systems are inextricably linked; as operational and digital technologies merge, cyber security (securing systems) and safety (the safety

---

[23] Dunn Cavalty, 2007: 14.

[24] Boin, 2017.

[25] Hon & Millard, 2018: 350.

[26] Michels & Walden, 2018: 32–37.

and reliability of systems) are intertwined. This creates new problems. For example, updates to operating systems and user software can have major unintended consequences for the functioning of systems in hospitals. That the damage caused by *WannaCry* involved missing updates is only half of the story (see inset). The other half is that the complex digital environments of organizations render updates time-consuming; updates entail risks that must first be explored before they can be implemented safely.

WannaCry and the UK's National Health Service[27]

The global ransomware attack known as *WannaCry* began on Friday, 12 May 2017. Within a day, it had affected over 230,000 computers in at least 150 countries. One of the most high-profile victims was the NHS in the UK. *WannaCry* exploited a known vulnerability in Windows, for which Microsoft had already released a patch 2 months earlier. The NHS had not yet implemented the patch; the malware spread mainly through the internal network of the affected hospitals.

WannaCry disrupted services in one-third of UK hospital trusts (around 80) and 8% of GP practices and NHS organizations (around 600 institutions). About 19,000 patient appointments were cancelled; 5 out of the 27 accident and emergency centres infected were unable to provide care to all patients and had to be relocated. Communication during the crisis also became more difficult because the use of e-mail was in many cases no longer possible. It took the NHS about 1 week to return to normal.

Estimates of the total financial damage caused by *WannaCry* worldwide range from a few hundred million to a staggering four billion dollars. The UK Department of Health and Social Affairs calculated the costs of the incident, broken down into costs incurred during the crisis and costs the following week, and into direct costs (lost production in terms of patient care) and the additional IT support needed to restore affected data and systems.

	During	Aftermath	Total
Direct costs	£19 million	0	£19 million
IT costs	£0.5 million	£72 million	£73 million
Total	£20 million	£72 million	£92 million

---

[27] Based on: https://www.nao.org.uk/report/investigation-wannacry-cyber-attack-and-the-nhs/# https://assets.publishing.service.gov.uk/government/uploads/system/uploads/attachment_data/file/747464/securing-cyber-resilience-in-health-and-care-september-2018-update.pdf

'Complex' means more than just 'complicated'. A complicated system consists of many parts and connections but is ultimately organized. A complex system consists of many parts and connections and, in part, lacks organization. Complex systems are characterized by multifaceted interactions that follow their own local rules; there are no overarching rules or principles that characterize the various interactions that can potentially take place.[28] If these interactions are closely aligned and tightly organized, disruption can have a significant external effect and lead to problems at the system level.[29]

This raises doubts about the current trend of linking all sorts of devices and systems to the internet without due regard for potential consequences, including for corporate and government systems, devices in hospitals, and physical infrastructure such as canal locks. Once they are connected to the internet, these systems are potentially vulnerable to errors and disruptions in other parts of the global infrastructure. This means that society is now vulnerable to unexpected system failures on a much larger scale.[30] The OECD notes that the 'indirect effects' of such errors or disruptions may lead to significant damage.[31]

Complexity becomes a problem if something goes wrong. An explosion may occur at the location where chemicals are mixed or where fireworks are stored; in terrorist attacks, the perpetrators are usually active on the ground or have left explosives there at an earlier stage. But in the disruption or failure of digital facilities, cause and effect may be far removed in physical terms. This makes it more difficult to determine causality, particularly when malicious actors are involved, and how and where authorities should act. Which organization should the authorities be looking at, and where? Which systems are involved and who is using them? It can also be unclear whether and under what circumstances a course of action, such as forcing entry into a system, will lead to disruption. The right moment to intervene is difficult to determine.

3.4   Geopolitics

Digitization has changed the position of countries in the world, especially countries with open societies. Digitization has increased their vulnerability, providing a much wider 'area of attack' for malicious actors. It has also given them the means to do serious damage, made even more attractive by the anonymity of the internet. Dependence on foreign providers also raises questions about the technological facilities that countries need to adequately guarantee the continuity of their core societal processes.

---

[28] West, 2017.

[29] Perrow, 1983.

[30] Clearfield & Tilcsik, 2018: 242.

[31] OECD, 2003: 45. Klaver et al. 2013 argue that the second and third-order effects of disruptions can be grave if they affect processes vital to other sectors and services.

3.4.1 Dependence on Large Foreign Providers

Especially in western countries, many organizations that provide these core services are privately owned. This is especially true of organizations that work with digital technology. The Dutch government largely depends on Fox-IT for the integrity and confidentiality of government information. For telecommunications services, the government relies on companies such as KPN. Due to such dependence, acquisitions are sensitive.[32] For example, the emergency number 112, the national communication network for emergency services (C2000), the Emergency Communication Facility, and the fibre optic network for defence and telecommunication services for Schiphol Airport would be potentially vulnerable to discontinuity if they were to be acquired by a provider from another country.[33] For many Fox-IT services, there is no alternative; the recent takeover of Fox-IT by a British party gives pause for thought.[34]

In addition to corporate takeovers, this issue also applies to tenders and investment in new technology. C2000 is currently maintained by an originally German company (Hytera) now in Chinese hands. The Chinese company Huawei is working with all major telecoms companies in the Netherlands and has many contracts in Europe to build 5G networks. There is suspicion that such companies are – with or without their knowledge – undermining Dutch society by enabling espionage, disruption or sabotage by other states. Some of the countries in which these companies are based have legislation that could force these firms to cooperate with their governments. Partly for this reason, the Dutch government decided in 2018 to phase out the use of Kaspersky's antivirus software.[35]

Particularly the growing presence of Chinese companies in EU member states is perceived as a risk to national economic security.[36] An underlying problem is that the internet is intrinsically insecure. Companies have an interest in an open and unsafe internet as this enables them to collect a great deal of user data.[37] But an open and unsafe internet also helps governments to undertake surveillance, often exploiting the lack of security in companies' existing systems, especially telecoms companies as they offer access to so much digital data traffic. China is certainly not the only country that intrudes into digital systems to collect information, with the ability to launch full-fledged cyber operations. The United States, France, Russia, the United Kingdom, Israel and Germany all have professional military cyber units and

---

[32] NCTV, 2018.

[33] Bulten et al., 2017: viii.

[34] Bulten et al., 2017; Van de Hoven van Genderen, 2017.

[35] https://www.rijksoverheid.nl/documenten/kamerstukken/2018/05/14/voorzorgsmaatregel-ten-aanzien-van-gebruik-kaspersky-antivirussoftware. Meanwhile, policy is being developed for secure software and hardware; see Ministry of Economic Affairs and Climate and Ministry of Justice and Security, 2018.

[36] AIVD, 2019.

[37] Schneier, 2018: 56–59; cf. Zuboff, 2019.

intelligence services with their own means of attack. Building up offensive cyber capacity is much cheaper and easier than aiming for a safer internet by, for example, investing in public interest technology or regulating vital infrastructure.[38] The net effect of building offensive cyber capacity is an increasingly unsafe digital realm.

3.4.2 *Malicious States*

Various actors have the capacity and motive to disrupt the core processes of society. Criminal actors and states constitute the leading threats to national security.[39] Criminals focus on where they can gain the most or have the greatest impact; increasingly, this means public services. In addition to major financial institutions, hospitals are increasingly targeted due to the sensitive personal data they possess and society's dependence on healthcare facilities and services. States tend to focus on espionage – with more than a hundred countries possessing the means for it – and the undermining of core processes in other societies. Of all malicious actors, states have the greatest resources at their disposal; they can choose specific goals, work on achieving them over long time horizons, and cause the greatest damage.

While the initial fear was that cyber weapons could destroy national electricity supplies or military command structures, they now appear to be aimed primarily at more mundane areas, often in pursuit of specific goals. Examples include the shutdown of the oil company Saudi Aramco in Saudi Arabia, the destruction of a blast furnace in Germany,[40] the paralysis of municipal computer systems in Atlanta, and the manipulation of elections. Such actions take place almost daily, not to destroy other countries but to disrupt their functioning and undermine citizen confidence. There are no international rules about what is permitted and about proportionate responses.[41] States are reluctant to help develop cyber-specific international rules of conduct. With their own activities in cyberspace often shrouded in secrecy, actions often go unanswered and continue unimpeded.

---

[38] For examples see: https://www.schneier.com/essays/archives/2019/02/public-interest_tech.html

[39] There is no generally accepted typology of malicious actors. It is also unclear what constitutes 'malicious'. NCTV, 2018 distinguishes between states, criminals, terrorists, hacktivists, cyber vandals and script kiddies, and insiders. This categorization is, in amended form, based on an extensive typology of threat actors by De Bruijne et al., 2017. Boundaries between these actors can be blurry as groups often work together and means of attack quickly become 'established' once they have been used.

[40] https://www.bsi.bund.de/SharedDocs/Downloads/DE/BSI/Publikationen/Lageberichte/Lagebericht2014.pdf?__blob=publicationFile, p. 31

[41] Mačák, 2017.

3.4.3   The Perfect Weapon

Digitization offers the opportunity for achieving major impact using relatively simple techniques, as seen in attacks on the core functions of the internet.[42] Such attacks can affect many sectors, making them an attractive first step in an escalating conflict. They are much cheaper and easier to carry out than attacks on specific organizations or networks, as they do not require access to the target system which can take months or years of preparation. Attacks can also be switched on and off with the touch of a button, making them highly effective means to exert pressure. Alarmingly, attacks on the core functions of the internet remain limited in discussions over national security and cyber conflict.[43]

Attacks on the Core Functions of the Internet: Dyn, Mirai and the Internet of Things

In 2016, the Domain Name System (DNS) was corrupted by a DDoS attack using the *Mirai* botnet.[44] With the failure of the little-known DNS provider Dyn, major platforms such as Twitter, Netflix, Reddit and many other popular websites and services were inaccessible in the US and Europe for most of the day. Thousands of compromised consumer devices from webcams to digital video recorders were enlisted in the attack. A similar attack later targeted major media websites in France.[45] Some consider the *Mirai* botnet attacks as a dress rehearsal.[46]

There have been many attacks on the DNS, including one on all 13 DNS root servers in 2002.[47] In 2015, China launched a 5-day DDos attack on Github for hosting websites that bypassed its censorship restrictions – the first time a state used its own digital infrastructure for offensive purposes. Also in 2015, hackers attacked Turkey's top-level DNS (.tr), rendering all websites using the domain name – banks, media companies, all government organizations and military networks – inaccessible for at least a day. That attack lasted for more than 2 weeks. Attacks on the DNS are difficult to mitigate because they mimic normal user behaviour and are difficult to separate from normal internet traffic.

---

[42] WRR, 2015, section 2.

[43] Snyder, 2017 provides a comprehensive overview of possible disruptions of the internet's core functions, with many examples; cf. Van Ruijven & Duijnhoven, 2018.

[44] https://en.wikipedia.org/wiki/2016_Dyn_cyberattack

[45] ENISA, 2018a: 50.

[46] Scott & Spaniel, 2016.

[47] DeNardis, 2014: 98.

Cyber weapons seem to be the 'perfect weapon'.[48] They can be obtained cheaply and used for myriad purposes, from disrupting organizations that provide services essential to the everyday functioning of society to sowing uncertainty and dissatisfaction. What is more, it is easy to cover one's tracks.[49] These features have led to a shift in the balance of power, with smaller countries now exercising more clout through the digital domain, able to take part in the global battlefield even if they lack the wherewithal to enter into large-scale military confrontation. Cyber-attacks such as *NotPetya* and *WannaCry* have also shown that the alleged perpetrators (Russia and North Korea, respectively) are prepared to accept a great deal of collateral damage.[50]

3.5   Conclusion

We can draw a number of conclusions:

- There is a very high degree of interdependence between the digital domain and the physical domain. Developments such as 'datafication', the use of algorithms in decision-making, and the complex web of connections between systems around the world mean that the physical realm now merges seamlessly with the digital realm. Societal disruption will increasingly have both a digital and a physical dimension.
- The continuity of everyday life has traditionally been a major public interest. In a digitized society, this interest remains undiminished.
- Digitization means that society is now vulnerable to new forms of disruption due to unstable and often poorly secured software and hardware as well as complex, cross-border supply and production chains. These create many opportunities for malicious actors to disrupt societal processes or even to take them down entirely.
- Digitization also means that the continuity of core societal processes at the national level largely depends on parties based overseas, specifically major providers of digital services and malicious state actors that specifically target these services.

---

[48] Sanger, 2018.

[49] ENISA, 2017.

[50] The Stuxnet attack on nuclear power stations in Iran, attributed to Israel and the United States, led to great collateral damage. Around 50,000 computers were infected in India, Indonesia, Pakistan and Germany. See Schneier, 2015: 150.

References

AIVD (Algemene Inlichtingen en Veiligheidsdienst) [General Intelligence and Security Service]. (2019). *Annual report 2018*. AIVD.

Boin, R. A. (2017). *De grenzeloze crisis: Uitdagingen voor politiek en bestuur* [Crisis without borders: Challenges for politics and management]. Inaugural lecture, Leiden University.

Broeders, D. (2017). Aligning the international protection of 'the public core of the internet' with state sovereignty and national security. *Journal of Cyber Policy, 2*(3), 366–376.

Bulten, C., de Jong, B., Breukink, E., & Jettinghoff, A. (2017). *Vitale vennootschappen in veilige handen* [Vital companies in safe hands]. Radboud Business Law Institute. https://www.wodc.nl/binaries/2609_Volledige_Tekst_tcm28-250320.pdf

Clearfield, C., & Tilcsik, A. (2018). *Meltdown: Why our systems fail and what we can do about it*. Penguin.

CPB [Netherlands Bureau for Economic Policy Analysis]. (2018). *Risk report on cyber security economy 2018*. https://www.cpb.nl/sites/default/files/omnidownload/CPB-Notitie-15okt2018-Risicorapportage-Cyberveiligheid-Economie-2018.pdf

De Bruijne, M., van Eeten, M., Gañán, C.H., & Pieters, W. (2017). *Towards a new cyber threat actor typology: A hybrid method for the NCSC Cyber Security Assessment*. https://www.wodc.nl/binaries/2740_Volledige_Tekst_tcm28-273243.pdf

DeNardis, L. (2014). *The global war for internet governance*. Yale University Press.

Dunn Cavalty, M. (2007). Critical information infrastructure: Vulnerabilities, threats and responses. *ICTs and International Security, 3*. https://www.peacepalacelibrary.nl/ebooks/files/UNIDIR_pdf-art2643.pdf

ENISA. (2017). *Commonality of risk assessment language in cyber insurance. Recommendations on cyber insurance*. https://www.enisa.europa.eu/publications/commonality-of-risk-assessment-language-in-cyber-insurance

ENISA. (2018a). *ENISA threat landscape report 2017: 15 top cyberthreats and trends*. ENISA.

ENISA. (2018b). *Good practices on interdependencies between OES and DSPs*. ENISA.

Hon, W. K., & Millard, C. (2018). Banking in the cloud. Part 2: regulation of cloud as 'outsourcing'. *Computer Law & Security Review, 34*, 337–357.

Kitchin, R. (2014). *The data revolution: Big data, open data, data infrastructures and their consequences*. Sage.

Klaver, M. H. A., Verheesen, B., & Luiijf, H. A. M. (2013). *Intersectorale afhankelijkheden: Buitenlandse methoden en mogelijke toepasbaarheid in Nederland* [Intersectoral dependencies: Methods from abroad and their possible application in the Netherlands]. TNO.

Luiijf, E., & Kernkamp, A. (2015). *Sharing cyber security information: Good practice stemming from the Dutch public-private participation approach*. TNO.

Mačák, K. (2017). From cyber norms to cyber rules: Re-engaging states as law-makers. *Leiden Journal of International Law, 30*(4), 877–899.

Michels, J. D., & Walden, I. (2018). How safe is safe enough? Improving cybersecurity in Europe's critical infrastructure under the NIS Directive. *Queen Mary School of Law Legal Studies Research Paper No. 291/2018*. https://ssrn.com/abstract=3297470

Ministry of Economic Affairs and Climate and Ministry of Justice and Security. (2018). *Roadmap Veilige Hard- en Software* [Roadmap for safe hardware and software]. The Hague.

Mueller, M. (2017). *Will the internet fragment? Sovereignty, globalization and cyberspace*. Polity Press.

NCTV. (2018). *Nationale veiligheid bij overnames en investeringen of inkoop en aanbesteding* [National security in take-overs and investments or service provision and tenders]. https://www.nctv.nl/binaries/WEB_113154_NCTV_Veiligheid_bij_overnames_tcm31-334520.pdf

Netherlands Court of Audit. (2019). *Digitale dijkverzwaring: Cybersecurity en vitale waterwerken* [Digital flood defences: Cyber security and vital defences]. The Hague.

OECD. (2003). *Emerging Risks in the 21st Century. An agenda for Action*. OECD Publishing.

Perrow, C. (1983). The organizational context of human factors engineering. *Administrative Science Quarterly, 28*(4), 521–541.

Pras, A. (2014). *Alle dagen internet. Beheersen door beheren* [Every day on the internet: Control through management]. Inaugural lecture, University of Twente.

Sanger, D. A. (2018). *The perfect weapon: War, sabotage and fear in the cyber age.* Crown.

Schneier, B. (2015). *Data and goliath: The hidden battles to collect your data and control your world.* W.W. Norton & Company.

Schneier, B. (2018). *Click here to kill everybody: Security and survival in a hyper-connected world.* W.W. Norton & Company.

Scott, J., & Spaniel, D. (2016). *Rise of the machines: The Dyn attack was just a practice run.* Institute for Critical Infrastructure Technology. https://icitech.org/wp-content/uploads/2016/12/ICIT-Brief-Rise-of-the-Machines.pdf

Snyder, C. (2017). *Too connected to fail. How attackers can disrupt the global internet, why it matters and what we can do about it.* Cyber Security Project, Belfer Center for Science and International Affairs.

Stratix. (2017). *Telekwetsbaarheid. Handelingsperspectief voor huishoudens bij uitval van telecomdiensten door stroomstoring* [Remote vulnerability. How households can respond in the event of an outage of telecom services due to a power outage]. Hilversum.

Van den Hoven van Genderen, R. (2017). Is de verkoop van Fox-IT aan een buitenlandse partij (de 'FOXIT') een bedreiging voor de nationale veiligheid? [Is the sale of Fox-IT to a foreign party (the 'FOXIT') a threat to national security?]. *Tijdschrift voor Internetrecht, 2017*(2).

Van Eeten, M., & Bauer, M. (2012). Mega-crises and the internet: risks, incentives, and externalities. In I. Helsoot, A. Boin, B. Jacobs, & L. Comfort (Eds.), *Mega-crises: Understanding the prospects, nature, characteristics and the effects of cataclysmic events.* Charles C. Thomas.

Van Eeten, M., Nieuwenhuijs, A., Luiijf, E., Klaver, M., & Cruz, E. (2011). The state and the threat of cascading failure across critical infrastructures: the implications of empirical evidence from media incident reports. *Public Administration, 89*(2), 381–400.

Van Gompel, M. (2018) Softwarefout en winkeldief oorzaak van grote treinstoring Amsterdam [Software error and shoplifter cause of major train failure Amsterdam]. *SpoorPro Professional Journal for the Rail Sector.* https://www.spoorpro.nl/materieel/2018/08/22/grote-treinstoring-in-amsterdam-door-softwarefout-en-winkeldief/

Van Ruijven, Th., & Duijnhoven, H. (2018). *Verkenning ten behoeve van de risicocategorie aantasting functioneren internet* [Exploration of the 'effects on the functioning of the internet' risk category]. TNO.

Van Ruijven, Th., & Keijser, B. (2017). *Ketenweerbaarheid tegen cyberdreigingen: uitgangspunten, good practices en een stappenplan voor het vergroten van cyber-ketenweerbaarheid* [Chain resilience against cyber threats: Principles, good practices and a step-by-step plan for improving cyber resilience]. TNO.

West, G. (2017). *Scale: The universal laws of growth, innovation, sustainability, and the pace of life in organisms, cities, economies, and companies.* Penguin.

WRR [Netherlands Scientific Council for Government Policy]. (2011). *iOverheid* [iGovernment]. Amsterdam University Press. https://www.wrr.nl/publicaties/rapporten/2011/03/15/ioverheid

WRR [Netherlands Scientific Council for Government Policy]. (2015). *De publieke kern van het internet. Naar een buitenlands internetbeleid* [The public core of the internet. Towards a foreign internet policy]. Amsterdam University Press. https://english.wrr.nl/publications/reports/2015/10/01/the-public-core-of-the-internet

WRR [Netherlands Scientific Council for Government Policy]. (2017). *Veiligheid in een wereld van verbindingen* [Security in a connected world]. WRR. https://www.springer.com/gp/book/9783030376055

Zuboff, S. (2019). *The age of surveillance capitalism: The fight for a human future at the new frontier of power.* PublicAffairs.

Chapter 4
Preparing for Digital Disruption

4.1 Introduction

Prevention is better than cure, goes the adage. There is much to be said for prevention, especially when there is a chance to avoid the consequences of disruption altogether. But even if we take every preventive measure under the sun, we can never entirely exclude the possibility of serious disruption to the normal functioning of society. We therefore need to be prepared and to have early-warning mechanisms that can alert us when things are going awry. If disruption does occur, adequate follow-up action is vital. Recovery and reconstruction are key if society is to resume its normal functioning as rapidly as possible.

For physical risks such as major flooding or a severe flu epidemic, the government and other actors have identified measures to increase preparedness, detect early signs of disruption, minimize the impact and facilitate recovery. Probably more than any other event, the Covid-19 outbreak has underlined the importance of swift and coordinated responses. The Dutch government, however, has only recently recognized the risk of societal disruption due to the failure or disruption of digital infrastructure. Partly for this reason, we are unprepared. Extant policies focus on cyber security and prevention rather than on handling disruptive events as they unfold. This section discusses how our plans for digital disruption could be designed to include better preparation for its effects on society. We distinguish between four stages: preparedness, detection, mitigation, and finally, recovery and reconstruction.

© The Author(s) 2021
E. Schrijvers et al., *Preparing for Digital Disruption*, Research for Policy,
https://doi.org/10.1007/978-3-030-77838-5_4

4.2   Preparedness

Detection, mitigation and, in particular, recovery and reconstruction largely depend on how well we are prepared to handle societal disruption. Unlike prevention, they involve measures that seek to limit the effects of the disruption and to facilitate recovery. They are comparable to the role played by firebreaks in a forest or artificial hills in flood defences, which do not prevent flooding but provide protection from the rising waters and limit the number of victims. Precautionary measures can likewise limit the societal disruption caused by 'digital fires'. The first stage is preparedness. Within this category, we distinguish between four areas: fall-back options, isolation, cyber security exercises, and the provision of information.

4.2.1   Fall-Back Options

Options for switching to different facilities come in many shapes. The most well-known is the back-up facility, a diesel generator to generate power in an emergency. A crucial issue is how long this type of facility would have to function. With back-up facilities for digital systems, one consideration is how long data needs to be retained, which would depend on the type of data involved. Following the *NotPetya* attack, Maersk was able to save much of its data by contacting data centres around the world. But what was missing was a back-up of how the company's own IT system – the digital core of the company – was set up.[1] The Maersk case shows the importance of companies to plan ahead. Some processes have become so large and complex that back-up facilities are practically impossible to implement, partly due to cost. In short, back-up facilities are important but are no longer the obvious solution for certain processes.

Another possibility when considering fall-back options is using multiple providers, applications or infrastructures so that contingency options are available. But this is not always feasible. There is no real alternative to the global internet, where the only realistic approach is a long-term joint effort by national governments, companies, non-governmental organizations and experts to make the internet more secure.[2] Another hurdle for having multiple contingency options is the poorly functioning market for digital services and products, particularly in the field of cyber security.[3] The result is that governments, companies and organizations worldwide must choose between a handful of large providers.[4] Precisely because of their size and importance, these providers are attractive targets for geopolitically motivated attacks. At the same time, they have become 'too big to fail' for major sections of the global economy.

---

[1] Maersk was able to restore this system through sheer chance. One of its terminals in Ghana had been down during the incident due to a local power outage. This terminal escaped the *NotPetya* attack, allowing Maersk to make a copy of the system. See Greenberg, 2018.

[2] WRR, 2015; Mueller, 2017.

[3] Overvest et al., 2018.

[4] The three largest Dutch banks depend on the services of the security company Akamai. See Overvest et al., 2018.

That said, concentration also has advantages when it comes to limiting disruption. Precisely due to their scale, large cloud providers are often better protected against cyber-attacks than the organizations that use them to host their data. With economies of scale, the services of these providers are often cheaper than those of smaller parties. At the same time, customers need to be confident that these giants are taking adequate measures to handle disruption. If many customers simultaneously face the same problem, questions will inevitably arise about who gets priority. The outage of Google Cloud (see Sect. 4.1) showed that Google had all kinds of contingency plans in place. The question is to what extent these plans are consistent with the public interests that the government represents.

An alternative fall-back option would be returning to more 'old-fashioned' ways of working. In the event of disruption or the failure of digital facilities, organizations are usually still able to temporarily revert to less efficient modes of working through paper-based methods or the manual operation of mechanical installations. But this assumes that employees are still *able* to work with these older systems, and that those systems remain available. The rise of digitization and robotics has meant that manual skills and 'old-fashioned' facilities (such as local bank branches), and even cash itself, are rapidly disappearing. Preparedness implies that alternative methods and skills to assure crucial societal functions remain available. An illustrative example comes from the US Navy, which has decided to teach recruits how to navigate by the stars again.[5]

4.2.2   Isolation

Firebreaks are used in forests to contain large fires. In the event of a nuclear disaster, the reactor is encased in a concrete shell to minimize radiation leaking into the environment. For every form of disruption, there are strategies for containing the incident and preventing the damage from spreading. For digital disruption, network separation could play this role. Network separation entails placing partitions between different systems and the digital processes that handle these systems. The most radical form of network separation is for an organization to disconnect from the global internet, known as 'islanding' among IT experts. But in a highly connected world, this is not always realistic.[6] After all, these systems are connected for a reason, and islanding deprives them of this connectedness.[7] The partial separation or temporary deactivation of specific networks are more attractive options.

When implemented properly, network separation can stop disruption in its tracks or prevent further contamination. Network separation is desirable for certain key societal functions, also because it reduces dependence on third parties. Nevertheless, most government organizations currently lack clear strategies for network separation and there is limited coordination. Organizations often independently decide on the form and extent of network separation. Departments are often reluctant to set requirements due to the additional costs.[8]

---

[5] Mentioned in Snyder, 2017.
[6] WRR, 2017: 21.
[7] Boin, 2017: 9–10.
[8] Geer et al., 2003.

4.2.3   Cyber Security Exercises

At the national level, within the European Union and in the context of NATO, cyber security exercises focus on critical infrastructure. There are also sectoral initiatives such as in the telecommunications, water, and financial sectors. Cyber security exercises give us a more realistic picture of the form disruption could take and its potential consequences.[9] They also enable parties to identify risks and hazards, familiarize themselves with emergency procedures and practise taking decisions under duress. An additional goal is strengthening mutual trust, essential when responding to an emergency.[10]

The number of cyber security exercises rose sharply worldwide between 2002 and 2015.[11] They increasingly involve a mixed group of private and public organizations (see inset).

Cyber Security Exercises for Financial Institutions[12]
The TIBER (Threat Intelligence-Based Ethical Red Teaming) initiative launched by the Netherlands' Central Bank (DNB) tests connectivity within the financial sector. It is a public-private partnership that includes, among others, the police, the National Coordinator for Security and Counterterrorism, banks, insurance companies, pension funds and the stock exchange.

TIBER focuses on simulating cyber-attacks on financial institutions, with ethical hackers copying the working methods of real hackers. Following the test, both the attacker and the bank provide crucial information about the resilience of digital security. Lessons learnt can be used to benefit the entire financial sector.

According to DNB, the TIBER test programme is an example of successful cooperation in the field of cyber security and could also be applied in other key sectors. A pilot programme is currently taking place in the energy sector in collaboration with the Cyber Security Alliance.

While the majority of cyber exercises take place in Europe, they do not cover all key sectors. Some exercises do not focus on digital infrastructure at all.[13] Exercises that involve multiple organizations, focusing on the complex chains and networks within which they operate, are few in number. But such exercises are vital, not only to identify dependencies, but to gain better insight into the various standards and protocols that organizations use. Cyber security exercises help organizations to learn how others respond and who should be approached in common situations.[14]

---

[9] Lawson, 2013; Bergstrom et al., 2016.

[10] Boeke, 2016.

[11] ENISA, 2015: 22–23.

[12] https://www.dnb.nl/en/news/news-and-archive/DNBulletin2018/dnb379565.jsp.   See   also: https://www.ecb.europa.eu/paym/cyber-resilience/tiber-eu/html/index.en.html

[13] See e.g. Netherlands Court of Audit, 2019: 9.

[14] EPSC, 2017.

4.2.4 Provision of Information

Another way of mitigating the effects of digital disruption is to provide information about what is happening and how to best respond. What constitutes useful information varies. Organizations affected by disruption need to know what actions they can take to limit the impact as much as possible. For instance, there are detailed communication requirements for the failure of electronic payment transactions, designed to help restore confidence.[15] Emergency services must have eyes on the ground; members of the public must know about first aid, emergency escape routes, and how to notify the authorities. The digital equivalent would include providing information about the installation of patches and about additional measures to reduce the risks of being affected.

The provision of information to citizens merits particular attention. During and immediately after societally disruptive events, citizens are often seen saving themselves and assisting others.[16] But the longer a disruptive situation lasts, the more it affects people's capacity to respond rationally. Little can be done about this. Research shows that citizens hardly ever prepare for disruptive events. They generally underestimate the likelihood of disruption or believe the consequences will be manageable. While people attach great importance to the government's response to crisis situations,[17] many governments prioritize asking citizens to take preventive measures. Information on coping with and responding to digital disruption is largely absent.[18]

Digital channels and social media can play key roles in crisis communication.[19] As almost everyone is connected to everyone else, people can be informed of disruptive events very quickly, even in real time, and be advised on how to get back to their normal daily business. Of course it is not only the government that uses social media: citizens communicate about incidents among themselves, sharing pictures and video clips, as happened during the attack on the Boston Marathon in 2013.[20] Social media can also be a highly disruptive factor in crisis communication. In the event of an incident, it is often members of the public who occupy 'front-row seats', broadcasting what they are witnessing to large numbers of other people and giving

---

[15] https://www.dnb.nl/binaries/Joint%20Forum%20High%20Level%20Principles%20for%20 Businss%20Continuity_tcm46-145518.pdf?2019070914

[16] Helsoot & Ruitenberg, 2004.

[17] Donahue et al., 2014.

[18] Frerks, 2018. On https://crisis.nl/wees-voorbereid/cyberaanval/, the Dutch government advises citizens about what to do before, during and after a cyber-attack. The advice for before and after an attack mainly concerns IT-related measures such as the use of antivirus software and changing passwords. The European Commission states that 'Providing the public with information on how they can mitigate at user and organizational level the effects of an incident could be an effective measure to mitigate a large-scale cybersecurity incident or crisis', illustrating how the provision of information still needs work in member states.

[19] Simon et al., 2015.

[20] Cassa et al., 2013.

their own, often emotional, account of events. If an incident were to disrupt or take out digital channels of communication, this would – in a society accustomed to rapid digital communication – only exacerbate people's feelings of unease. It has become extremely challenging for governments to maintain the upper hand in providing information. In cross-border cyber incidents, EU member states only coordinate their public communications to a very limited extent.

4.3   Detection and Early-Warning Systems

The early detection of disruptive events is important because the longer the signs go unnoticed, the greater the potential for damage.[21] Early detection can take many possible forms, including the monitoring of networks and data flows; this approach is mainly technical in nature and will not be considered in detail here. We turn to the sharing of information between parties, an effective means to guarantee the performance and continuity of key sectors.[22] How this is organized and the development of a strategic information position are important factors.

4.3.1   Organizing the Exchange of Information

The exchange of information in many countries is organized through public-private partnerships. At the European level, the European Union Agency for Cyber Security (ENISA) and the European Computer Response Team (Cert-EU) are the primary information node and centre of expertise, representing the institutions of the European Union in numerous national and international forums. At the state level, National Cyber Security Centres fulfil similar functions, serving as the Computer Security Incident Response Team for national governments and critical service providers.

In the Netherlands, the exchange of information between government bodies and public and private actors has become much more comprehensive. Digital processes such as the government's electronic message service and the identification and authentication of citizens and companies wishing to use government services have been designated as critical services. The implementation of the Network and Information Security (NIS) Directive means that internet exchange points, top-level domain name registries and DNS service providers fall under this regime.[23] The NIS

---

[21] EPSC, 2017: 4.

[22] Settanni et al., 2017; Luiijf & Kernkamp, 2015; Choo, 2011.

[23] The NIS Directive applies to essential services rather than to key processes. Organizations that fall within these three categories provide a service essential to the continuity of critical and/or key economic activities. The provision of the service depends on network and data systems, and an incident would have a significant disruptive effect on the provision of that service.

Directive obliges major digital service providers to report incidents and to take measures to manage risks and reduce the consequences of incidents.[24] Although this extension of legislation is an important step, questions remain about the structure of the current system.[25] While the exchange of information is largely organized along sectoral lines, digitized societal processes are often interconnected, meaning any disruption could be accompanied by cascade effects between sectors. A quick and effective response to disruption would require the exchange of information not only within sectors but between them.[26]

The exchange of information is also hampered by the distinction between 'critical providers' and 'non-critical providers'. While critical providers exchange information with each other and with the government through Information Sharing Analysis Centres, many organizations classified as critical use the services of parties whose products and services are *not* classified as critical. The latter are not bound by the same reporting obligations as critical providers, although their operations may have a major impact on the continuity of critical processes (see inset).

Power Supply Under Pressure from Digitization[27]

The electricity system is classified as critical infrastructure in almost every country. Because this system increasingly relies on digital technology, any issues with digital technology could have a major impact on the supply of power. Yet the suppliers of digital technology are often not required to meet the same safety and security requirements as providers of critical services.

Advanced software and algorithms play a growing role in the supply, transport, and distribution of electricity. This trend is introducing new vulnerabilities. The risk of outages due to programming errors increases because processes in power plants and electricity networks are controlled by increasingly complex software programs. Disruption can also occur if autonomous digital systems behave in unexpected ways and/or respond to one another in unexpected ways – a risk with pre-programmed systems for energy production and supply from solar panels and wind turbines. Our digitized electricity system is also vulnerable to deliberate disruption, particularly now that many parts of the system are connected to the internet.

Because more and more societal functions depend on electricity, the consequences of incidents are likely to be more serious. And because the power supply of many European countries is now interlinked, vulnerabilities in the electricity system of one country also pose risks to the electricity systems of other countries.

---

[24] This includes online marketplaces, search engines and cloud service providers.

[25] For references to critical reports, see CSR, 2017: 3.

[26] Cf. CSR, 2017: 6.

[27] Based on Council for the Environment and Infrastructure, 2018: 14–19. Cf. ENISA for further vulnerabilities to cyber-attacks: https://www.enisa.europa.eu/publications/power-sector-dependency

The question is to what extent the current distinction between 'critical' and 'non-critical' providers should be retained. The same question arises for the critical and non-critical parts of government, because information flows transcend the departmental boundaries and levels of government.[28]

The distinction between critical and non-critical processes also affects businesses and societal organizations. While companies and organizations deemed non-critical receive less information about vulnerabilities, they often fulfil key societal functions such as supplying medicines or checking the quality of drinking and swimming water.[29] To bridge this gap in the Netherlands, the Digital Trust Centre has been set up as a counterpart to the Information Sharing Analysis Centres for the private sector. But the companies served by the Digital Trust Centre vary enormously in the information they need, their ability to take remedial measures, and the potential impact on society of any disruption in their functioning. The same problem exists in other countries. The British Cyber Security Strategy identifies a number of 'preferential sectors' in addition to 13 vital sectors, on the grounds that 'other companies and organizations' also need more support.[30]

Although information sharing has improved significantly in recent years, the definition of society's core processes requires adjustment. As these processes are increasingly digitized and embedded in complex networks, clear distinctions between 'critical' and 'non-critical' processes can no longer be made; nor will measures solely targeting critical processes necessarily improve our security. There are so many 'unknown unknowns' that it is impossible to know in advance exactly which processes or outages would lead to disruption.[31] The cross-border chains and networks within which critical providers operate necessitate international information sharing. We need a more strategic approach to information to better understand the dependencies involved.

4.3.2 Strategic Information

Cyber risks are relatively new and remain difficult to identify and evaluate. Nevertheless, important steps have been taken in recent years to share information on digital security measures, vulnerabilities and incidents.[32] We know, for instance, that every piece of commercial software has many vulnerabilities, the majority of

---

[28] WRR, 2011a.

[29] For examples see: https://www.volkskrant.nl/nieuws-achtergrond/had-de-storing-van-112-voorkomen-kunnen-worden~b235b093/

[30] HM Government 2016. One criticism is that the more 'vital' processes are identified, the more complex the task of setting priorities becomes. See House of Lords, 2018.

[31] Boin, 2017; Carr, 2015.

[32] Hausken, 2007.

which have not yet been discovered.[33] In the meantime, vulnerabilities are also appearing in hardware (such as chips), meaning that it is possible to read the memory of computers without authorization.[34] The landscape of malicious actors is also constantly changing. All this means that the task of identifying potential issues and publicizing the available solutions is never finished. Given the global and sometimes geopolitical nature of the threats, robust international cooperation and the structural involvement of intelligence services are vital.

Our current level of information sharing on security measures, vulnerabilities and incidents is insufficient for an adequate detection system. There are too many gaps in our knowledge about the chains and networks through which digital disruption could spread. We need detailed insight into the interdependencies between companies and organizations involved in society's core processes, the importance of which are often underestimated.[35] The potential effects of disruption further down the chain currently remain outside of risk analyses and crisis plans.

Understanding these dependencies requires analysis from an international perspective.[36] While attacks often exploit generic vulnerabilities, incidents may affect European member states in different ways. The services of EU member states may be interdependent, meaning that incidents in one country can impact other countries, as seen for example in international payment traffic. Attackers' use of networks to achieve their goals also means disruptions will have wider reach.

More knowledge is also required about the government's strategic position. What crisis-management options are available? What dependencies would the government have to contend with? Most providers of critical services are privately owned and do not fall under direct government control; many are based overseas. What authority would the government have over such parties? The context in which the government must operate is affected by market concentration and foreign ownership. Although the risk of (foreign) share ownership is adequately contained in many sectors, it remains a key concern for critical infrastructure.[37] As critical processes are digitized, the same applies to dependence on (foreign) private digital service providers, such as cloud providers. Looking ahead, decisions will need to be made about investments in new digital technology. If the government does not anticipate developments early and seek to manage them, it may become more difficult to manage digital disruptions when they occur.

---

[33] According to Schneier (2015: 145–146), there are hundreds or even thousands of vulnerabilities. Pupillo et al., 2018 arrive at a much lower number (at least 14 vulnerabilities in an average software program).

[34] See for example: https://techcrunch.com/2018/05/01/what-do-meltdown-spectre-and-ryzenfall-mean-for-the-future-of-cybersecurity/?guccounter=1

[35] NCTV, 2018; Klaver et al., 2013: 56; CSR, 2017.

[36] ENISA, 2018: 21.

[37] Bulten et al., 2017: viii.

4.3.3   Responsibilities

Experience suggests that security within sectors does not improve unless the government takes a clear lead. But in complex, networked societies and economies, security also requires collective commitment from all parties involved.[38] Here the responsibility of the government is to create the conditions which ensure the effective sharing of information. At the same time, the government should encourage, and sometimes require, market actors to take their responsibilities seriously and to develop the necessary capabilities to do this. The government has traditionally played this role to ensure the continuity of core societal processes. Their digitization means that the government must play this role in the digital domain as well.

Sharing and analysing information is necessary to improve the cyber security of organizations, to make them more resilient to incidents, and to limit the damage when incidents occur. But not all parties currently participate in the Information Sharing Analysis Centres. Some are reluctant to share sensitive information in light of competition, legal restrictions, national security, and the government's ability to use it for law enforcement purposes.[39] Such reluctance may be greater during a crisis with reputational damage at stake.[40] Nevertheless, security must be everyone's priority.[41] The challenge is for the government to improve its position without jeopardizing security, confidentiality and the systematic sharing of information. The EU's Network and Information Security Directive provides the tools for this by imposing stricter requirements on critical providers for reporting incidents.[42] But we still do not know enough about how this will be supervised, or about the consequences for violating the trust on which the sharing of information is based.[43]

4.4   Responding to Incidents

Digital processes have been affected by incidents large and small in recent years. Incidents in the Netherlands have been handled successfully, in that they did not lead to widespread societal disruption. This may tempt us to conclude that current instruments and regulations are adequate. But the continuing march of

---

[38] WRR, 2012.

[39] Koepke, 2017.

[40] Bharosa et al., 2010.

[41] Van Vollenhoven, 2018: 80.

[42] There are a number of reporting obligations. See Sect. 4.5.

[43] Luiijf and Kernkamp (2015: 18) argue that relationships based on trust should be regulated through rewards (in the form of information from other parties) as well as sanctions (withholding information).

digitization – particularly the growing interconnectedness of the digital and physical realms – encourages us to rethink existing frameworks and procedures. There are three specific areas where we need to reassess our existing instruments. We discuss them in turn below: legal powers, cross-border mitigation, and setting priorities.

4.4.1 Legal Powers

In the physical realm, the government has emergency services such as the police, fire brigade, ambulance and rescue teams to respond to crises. These and other services have legal powers to carry out their duties, for example the ability to cordon off particular locations, enter a company's premises or initiate an evacuation. But what resources can the government call on in the event of a digital crisis? The hack at DigiNotar in 2011 painfully revealed the government's dependence on private actors to resolve problems in the digital realm.

The Acquisition of DigiNotar[44]

On 29 August 2011, the government received a report of problems at the DigiNotar certificate authority, responsible for securing electronic communications from and between government bodies (known as Public Key Infrastructure or PKI). Hackers had managed to release forged DigiNotar certificates. As a result, government certificates could no longer be relied on and were possibly even unusable. Goods at the Port of Rotterdam could no longer be accepted, social security payments were blocked, and the payments system compromised.

The immediate reason for the impending crisis lay with the major browser suppliers, including Microsoft, which were losing confidence in all DigiNotar certificates, including the PKI government certificates. This was a very real threat as Microsoft could have blocked the use of all DigiNotar certificates with its monthly security update to maintain confidence in its own systems. Regardless of the parties involved, Microsoft did not want to continue supporting potentially unsafe communications.

At this point, the Dutch government had every interest in clarifying how many certificates had been manipulated or compromised. But despite urgent investigations, it was unable to retrieve this information. On 3 September, the government decided to take over the management of DigiNotar. There was no specific legal basis for this, but the Dutch government was able to count on the 'voluntary' cooperation of its American parent company Vasco. Microsoft then postponed its security update in the Netherlands for 1 week, which bought enough time to replace the certificates.

---

[44] Based on reports from the Dutch Safety Board 2012 and the Inspectorate of Justice and Security 2012 that evaluated the Diginotar incident.

Estonian Government and Gemalto[45]

The vulnerability in the chip of Estonian ID cards is a more recent example of the dependence of governments in solving problems in the digital realm. In September 2017, a vulnerability was discovered in a certificate that affected laptops and PCs as well as authentication to cloud applications. The vulnerability also affected ID cards in Estonia and eID cards in Slovakia, Spain and other countries. In Estonia, the ID card is used to authenticate one's person and to digitally sign documents. In theory, hackers were able to steal users' digital identity and access sensitive personal information, manipulate the results of e-voting, and hack into the state's information systems.

In November, the Estonian government decided to suspend all certificates of approximately 800,000 ID cards. Intensive users such as doctors were able to update their certificates at several government locations while the remote updating of certificates was disabled. Gemalto, the company that produced the chips, and the Estonian government, seeking €152 million in damages, traded accusations. The government was unhappy with Gemalto's handling of the security breach, especially its failure to notify the government of the problem.

At first glance, the Dutch decision-making structure for granting legal powers for crisis decision-making appears in good order. If societal disruption occurs, decisions are made through structures set out in the National Guide for Crisis Decision-Making (NHC). There is also a National ICT Crisis Plan, currently under review. In the NHC, the government has three roles: facilitation, management, and coordination. The latter, including the deployment of the police and fire brigade, and requisitioning resources, requires legal authority. The NHC also refers to 'measures in the event of a major IT incident' which are not set out in detail.[46]

The national IT Crisis Plan describes an IT crisis as 'a threat or crisis that originates in the field of information technology, which places one or more vital interests in jeopardy and for which the regular structures are not adequate.'

In the event of an (imminent) IT crisis, the IT Response Board (IRB) is activated. The IRB – a flexible public-private partnership – analyses the crisis and, if necessary, advises the Interdepartmental Crisis Management Committee, the official communication channel for the Ministerial Crisis Management Committee, chaired by the Minister of Justice and Security or the Prime Minister.

---

[45] See Ventsel and Madisson 2019 for a reconstruction of the Estonian case.
[46] The Dutch National ICT Crisis Plan includes nothing on this subject either.

Private actors can be required to cooperate if (imminent) disruption or the failure of their systems could undermine the public interest. They are required to keep the government informed about the situation and to cooperate in tackling the causes and consequences of the disruption.[47] But the interests of private organizations are not always consistent with the public interest that government represents; nor does the government have the means to force private parties headquartered overseas to cooperate. The government's role in cyber security is often limited to providing advice or assistance to the private organizations that form the critical infrastructure. Such was the case when, partly due to the lack of powers to intervene, the municipal crisis response team in Rotterdam was unable to access information about the terminals and systems of the container company Maersk as they were being hit by the *NotPetya* attack (see inset).

NotPetya and the Municipality of Rotterdam

In June 2017, hackers working for the Russian military distributed the *NotPetya* ransomware. One of the most prominent victims was Maersk, which runs container terminals around the world. The gates to ports could not be used, cranes ceased to work, trucks were unable to unload their cargo and new cargo shipments could not be booked. Maersk, an ultramodern shipping company, was forced to revert to a paper-based system.[48]

The terminals in the port of Rotterdam were affected by the attack. Container transport via the port as well as the surrounding highways and rail links ground to a halt, causing congestion and long traffic jams. The city authorities were unprepared. They had difficulty gathering the relevant actors; the municipal crisis response organization responsible for public order was initially denied information about Maersk's terminals and systems. The city authorities were thus unable to assess the situation's seriousness and whether, for example, there was a risk to public order.

Formal assistance from the National Coordinator for Security and Counterterrorism was impossible because Maersk's APM terminals, unlike the Port of Rotterdam itself, were not part of the 'critical infrastructure'.

A great deal of sector-specific legislation outlines the powers of the government in exceptional circumstances. During a crisis, parties are obliged to cooperate and to follow government instructions. The legislation, however, is lengthy and complex.[49] Extensive explanation would be needed for relevant parties to understand the implications. Although sectoral legislation can provide useful starting points for government intervention, the question is whether these powers are sufficiently comprehensive and suited to the problems of a digital world.

---

[47] Luiijf and Klaver (2015: 266) argue for direct access to the relevant IT systems of producers.

[48] Greenberg, 2018.

[49] Muller, 2014: 45.

The government can also act without making use of sector-specific provisions. In a crisis, and if circumstances warrant, the law could simply be broken in a case of 'needs must'. This is not a desirable course of action.[50] It would require a degree of improvisation, better minimized for maintaining the rule of law.[51] Government actions – especially interventions by authorities such as the police and the public prosecution service – should be predictable and subject to accountability.[52] A crucial question is whether interventions would be justified if they did not also serve the purposes of an investigation or prosecution.

The problem extends to who takes the relevant decisions and initiates the required actions. As in the physical realm, the primary responsibility of companies operating in the digital realm is to ensure their own security and to draw up contingency plans for emergencies. Large companies need to arrange for their own cyber security departments, sector-specific Computer Emergency Response Teams or employ the services of private cyber security companies.[53] The government will only step in when circumstances involve (the risk of) societal disruption.

It is often not immediately clear who or what caused an incident, and in the case of deliberate disruption, the motive.[54] It can thus be unclear whether government bodies such as the Ministry of Defence, the national cyber security authorities, the police or the intelligence services should take action. As each body has its own sets of powers and interests, the government's approach could well depend on who responds to the incident: the police are primarily concerned with identifying perpetrators so that the public prosecutor can take action; the intelligence services are more inclined to protect their information position; the national cyber security agency, given its remit to ensure information security, openness and stability, focuses on remedial action. While the police also have the powers to provide assistance and to prevent escalation, public order and security must be at stake.[55] A national cyber security authority would not always be bound by this requirement.

In conclusion, legal powers for the digital domain and for mitigating disruption are not always sufficiently clear and well defined. The emphasis is currently on advising and supporting parties within infrastructure categorized as critical. But if parties refuse to cooperate, it is unclear what powers the government has to intervene, and on what grounds. Given the limited powers of the national cyber security authority, which focuses on technical expertise and assistance, previous interventions have largely been ad hoc.

---

[50] Within the modernization of state emergency law, consideration is currently being given to supplementing existing emergency powers with specific powers over certain IT services. See: https://www.rijksoverheid.nl/documenten/kamerstukken/2018/07/03/tk-modernisatie-staatsnoodrecht

[51] See Kortmann, 2009.

[52] To obtain information, the Public Prosecutor can initiate a search warrant process in accordance with art. 96c Sv. See Prins, 2019: 721.

[53] For a similar argument, see Prins, 2012: 44–45.

[54] Prins, 2012: 45.

[55] Prins, 2019: 578.

4.4.2 Combating Cross-Border Crises

Digital disruption will unlikely be confined within national borders. Research shows that cross-border crises are by definition challenging.[56] Nevertheless, some steps have already been taken at the international level. For example, the EU has put various crisis management provisions in place, some specifically for cyber security.[57]

> The most important initiative is the Cyber Security Strategy of the European Union which dates from 2013, on which the 2016 Network and Information Security Directive and the 2018 Cyber Security Act are based. The NIS Directive obliges member states to establish a national centre for cyber security and establishes European level cooperation between these centres. The Cyber Security Act strengthens ENISA, the EU agency for cyber security.
>
> The EU has a number of specialist cyber security organizations, including ENISA, the European Centre for Cyber Crime (EC3), which falls under Europol, the European Defence Agency (EDA), and the European Computer Emergency Response Team (CERT-EU).
>
> A number of countries, including the Netherlands, have signed a letter of intent for a European Cyber Rapid Response Force to respond quickly in the event of a large-scale digital incident.[58]
>
> The Forum of Incident Response and Security Teams (FIRST) is a worldwide partnership of CERTs.

The capacity of these facilities has improved in recent years.[59] While cross-border initiatives have been initiated to improve cyber security in critical sectors, such as energy and transport,[60] existing mechanisms for dealing with cross-border crises are fragmented across a range of institutions. Their functions are not always clearly defined and, according to experts, their effectiveness is at best limited.[61] Although the NIS Directive should lead to improvements, it still does not provide a framework for EU-level cooperation in the case of major cyber incidents.[62] EU

---

[56] Boin & Lodge, 2018.

[57] Backman & Rhinard, 2018.

[58] https://eeas.europa.eu/topics/eu-international-cyberspace-policy/47525/new-tool-address-cyber-threats-eus-rapid-response-force_en. Compare the proposal for a European cyber agency in CEPS, 2018. This agency also has the authority to attribute attacks.

[59] https://www.enisa.europa.eu/news/enisa-news/csirts-and-incident-response-capabilities-in-europe

[60] European Commission, 2016.

[61] Boin & Lodge, 2018; cf. European Commission, 2016: 2.

[62] Implemented in the Netherlands through the Network and Information Systems Security Act (17 October 2018, Bulletin of Acts and Decrees 2018, 387). https://wetten.overheid.nl/BWBR0041515/2018-11-09

member states have therefore asked the European Commission to produce plans for responding to a major cyber incident involving multiple member states. In the meantime, the 'blueprint'[63] outlines what a timely and effective response would look like. Practice exercises are needed, and since the blueprint does not provide any new legal powers, combating incidents will still fall on national crisis management mechanisms. The question is whether these are still fit for purpose.

4.4.3   Setting Priorities

Not all instruments and resources can be deployed simultaneously. Some areas will have to be prioritized, again pointing to the importance of clearly defined decision-making powers. There are questions about when the government should deploy which instruments, the most effective use of resources, and the relationship between detecting and counteracting incidents on the one hand and legal powers on the other. Many governments are also working to improve the categorization of cyber incidents.

France is considering classifying cyber-attacks according to specific response options.[64] The United States has had such a system since 2014, where The National Cyber Security and Communications Integration Center (NCCIC) reports incidents and assesses risks by assigning a score between 1 and 100 based on 8 criteria:
actual impact on an organization;
observed activity;
location of detection;
actors involved;
type of information that has been lost, compromised or corrupted;
recovery options;
cross-sectoral dependencies;
extent of societal disruption.[65]

The United Kingdom has recently developed a system of six categories of incidents, covering the entire spectrum from local incidents to national emergencies. The British National Cyber Security Centre links each category to a party responsible for responding to the incident.[66]

---

[63] See http://ec.europa.eu/transparency/regdoc/rep/3/2017/NL/C-2017-6100-F1-NL-MAIN-PART-1.PDF. A blueprint is also attached to the document. See: http://ec.europa.eu/transparency/regdoc/rep/3/2017/NL/C-2017-6100-F1-NL-ANNEX-1-PART-1.PDF

[64] Secrétariat général de la défense nationale, 2018: 140.

[65] https://www.us-cert.gov/NCCIC-Cyber-Incident-Scoring-System and https://grants.nhisac.org/BackgroundData/Cyber_Incident_Severity_Schema.pdf

[66] https://www.ncsc.gov.uk/news/new-cyber-attack-categorisation-system-improve-uk-response-incidents

Following the EU blueprint for preventing incidents, the European NIS cooperation group[67] has drawn up a taxonomy of large-scale cyber incidents.[68] Alongside malicious acts, it includes spontaneous system failure, natural phenomena such as fires, floods and earthquakes, human error, and failures by third parties. The aim is to link this taxonomy to integrated EU political crisis response (IPCR) regulations.

While the Dutch government's assessment of incident severity is linked to its list of critical infrastructure, the examples above show the usefulness of additional criteria for combating digital incidents. For starters, the national government would not have to be involved in all incidents. A more differentiated classification system could form the basis for a more clearly defined division of responsibilities, both within the various layers of government (such as the national cyber security authority, government departments, safety regions, and municipal information security services) and between government bodies and the business community. A more nuanced classification system for cyber incidents would allow for more effective responses, as action by the central government would no longer have to be directly linked to incidents involving critical infrastructure.

Prioritization also needs to occur on the spot. In the event of a major fire, the fire brigade can choose to put out the fire or to minimize damage by keeping nearby buildings wet; adjacent buildings may suffer water damage, but would be salvaged. Something similar may apply to disconnecting digital systems, requiring the assessment of the risks of acute interruption to operations and the risks of problems spreading further, possibly leading to broader damage. Because many digital systems are in the hands of private parties, the considerations the government will consider when intervening must be clear in advance.

Prioritization involves both technical and substantive aspects. On the technical side, the logic of the systems will play a role. This means that decisions regarding connecting and disconnecting networks will be based on a particular sequencing; here it is essential to know how the various systems and organizations in a network are connected. In terms of content, there is the question of which processes should be kept operating the longest and be restarted first in the event of failure. The government's choices will not always be self-explanatory to all parties. Private actors may want to safeguard their own systems and those of their clients first, rather than prioritizing the public interest.

In the Netherlands, the continuity of critical processes is given priority in the event of an incident. Critical processes that fall under category A (the disruption of which would have severe economic and societal impact) are prioritized over those in category B (the disruption of which would have a more limited, but still

---

[67] The NIS cooperation group consists of representatives of EU member states, ENISA and the European Commission. It was established on the basis of Article 11 of the NIS Directive.

[68] http://ec.europa.eu/information_society/newsroom/image/document/2018-30/cybersecurity_incident_taxonomy_00CD828C-F851-AFC4-0B1B416696B5F710_53646.pdf

substantial economic and societal impact). Digitization challenges this categorization. For digital facilities, the current list of critical infrastructure focuses mainly on traditional telecommunications services and their role in for instance the deployment of emergency services and communication between emergency services. The telecoms/IT sectors, however, fall under category B. Whether this is sustainable is doubtful. Second only to the power supply, the failure of digital facilities would likely lead to the most significant cascade effects. There are detailed shutdown and recovery plans for electricity companies, with the restoration of public order and safety being priorities. No such plans are in place for digital disruption, again underlining the importance of rethinking our definition of critical processes.

4.5   Recovery & Reconstruction

The final phase in dealing with digital disruption concerns recovery and reconstruction – the resumption of normal functioning. If normal everyday life is seriously disrupted, various steps will be required to get things working normally again. Often things will not return to how they were before the disruption because people and organizations learn from the incident. Companies and organizations affected by a computer virus or ransomware, or which have experienced system and process failures for other reasons, often alter their policies (for example staff only using USB sticks under strict conditions). To learn from such incidents, we must analyse what went wrong. The recovery and reconstruction process also requires adequate facilities. This means, for example, that victims are compensated for damages. Learning lessons and providing compensation are to some extent related. Those who wish to redesign core societal processes must have the resources to do this.

4.5.1   Evaluating and Learning Lessons

The recovery and reconstruction phase must be used to reflect on how new digital facilities are to be embedded. This may extend to rethinking the balance between economic interests and political and administrative authority in the organization of the digital society. Changing priorities may mean developing facilities that privilege security over speed, efficiency, and low prices.

We need more than reorientation; past incidents must lead to concrete learning.[69] This often does not happen, even in the aftermath of major incidents such as *NotPetya* and *WannaCry*.[70] The availability of historical data on cyber incidents is limited; there is currently no generally accepted definition of what constitutes an incident.[71] An additional problem is that most data on incidents does not concern

---

[69] Van Vollenhoven, 2018.

[70] Van Tiel, 2019.

[71] Valeriano & Maness, 2018.

vulnerabilities that could lead to societal disruption. Public data on incidents tends to focus on data breaches because legal disclosure requirements focus on them.[72] The Network and Information Security Directive will change this by introducing a reporting obligation for problems that affect the continuity of 'essential services'. The European Payment Directive will also require payment service providers to report major incidents that jeopardize the financial interests of their users. As both reporting obligations have been introduced very recently, it is too early to draw meaningful conclusions.

As for the supervision of digital security, the Netherlands still lacks a designated supervisor.[73] Several organizations are active in specific, limited areas: the Data Protection Authority registers data breaches; De Nederlandsche Bank (the central bank) protects electronic payment transactions; the Telecommunications Agency monitors network providers. Several government departments are also involved as their remits cover critical sectors. The incident data that each of these organizations collects is only haphazardly shared and not always analysed, let alone in a coordinated manner.[74] This is a missed opportunity. Because digital disruptions always involve multiple organizations and sectors, it would be extremely useful to compare data on incidents.

4.5.2   Compensation

An important aspect of recovery and reconstruction is compensation to victims, whether through liability insurance or government payments. Adequate compensation reduces risks and damages to society[75] and contributes to the recovery of the economy, social stability and trust in institutions.[76] In principle, it is possible to insure against cyber risks.[77] As the market for cyber insurance is a fraction of the market for other risks, we may see considerable growth in this area.

Risks are insurable if they can be quantified in terms of their probability and impact. It must also be possible to draw on a sufficiently large group of individuals affected by the risk, who would therefore be willing to share it. Finally, risks need to be unpredictable in terms of when and where they materialize, and be beyond the control of the insured parties. Otherwise, each party would insure itself individually.

---

[72] OECD, 2017: 34. For an indication of the number of data breaches, see: https://autoriteitperson-aldata.nl/nl/onderwerpen/security/meldplicht-datalekken/Digits-datalekken-2018. The Dutch Data Protection Authority received more than 20,000 reports of data breaches in 2018. In 2017, there were 10,009 reports; in 2016, 5849 reports.

[73] This is a more general problem. See Van Vollenhoven, 2018.

[74] One exception is the National Coordinator for Security and Counterterrorism, which provides an overview of reports and incidents in an appendix to the Netherlands Cyber Security Assessment. See NCTV, 2019: 43–46.

[75] Bruggeman & Faure, 2018: 11; WRR, 2011b: 16, 53.

[76] Kuipers & Tjepkema, 2017.

[77] OECD, 2017; Biener et al., 2015.

Cyber risks are difficult to quantify due to lack of historical data. We have no clear method for classifying incidents and no insight into the resilience of companies and the types of losses they incur.[78] Cyber risks are also constantly evolving, complicating quantification. Insurers could face massive losses due to the accumulation of risks.[79] If many parties depend on the same infrastructure or suppliers, or use the same basic software, insurers will have difficulty pooling the risks across sectors or regions. Lloyd's and Cyence have estimated a cloud software service outage, depending on its duration, to cause between $4.6 billion and $53 billion in damages.[80] The accumulation of risks is a major reason the market for cyber insurance is growing so slowly. The extensive damage (see table below) and damage claims resulting from *NotPetya* are additional reasons for large insurers to limit their coverage of cyber incidents.

Impact of Interruption to Business Operations Due to the NotPetya Incident[81]

Organisation	Commercial Impact	Financial Components	Source
A.P. Moller – Maersk	$250-300 million	Earnings Reduction	Q4 2017 Financials
Beiersdorf AG	Minimal sales impact €15 million	€35 million sales shifted Q2 to Q3 Additional expenses	Q2 2017 Financials Q4 2017 Earnings Call
FedEx (TNT Express)	$400 million	Earnings Reduction	Q4 2018 Financials
Merck & Co.	$410 million $380 million	2017, 2018 Sales Reduction Additional Expenses	Q4 2017 Financials Q3 2018 Financials
Mondelez International	-$104 million $84 million	2017 Sales Reduction Additional Expenses	Q4 2017 Earnings Call Q4 2017 Earnings Release
Nuance Communications	$68 million $31.2 million	2017 Sales Reduction Additional Expenses	Q3 2018 Financials
Reckitt Benckiser	-£114 million	2% Q2 Sales Reduction 2% Q3 Sales Reduction	Press Release Q2 2017 Financials Q3 2017 Financials
Saint-Gobain	-€220-250 million €80 million	2017 Sales Reduction 2017 Earnings Reduction	Q3 2017 Earnings Release Q1 2018 Earnings Release

These insurance companies felt emboldened by the United States' attribution of the cyber-attack to Russia.[82] They also explicitly excluded alternative cover from their policies, for example through liability for or damage to company equipment (so-called 'silent cyber').

---

[78] OECD, 2017; ENISA, 2017; Nieuwesteeg et al., 2017. Many insurance policies focus on the loss of customer data and not on the cost of repairing digital infrastructure and losses due to disruption of business.

[79] OECD, 2017: 123.

[80] Lloyd's & Cyence, 2017.

[81] AON, 2019: 8. Based on corporate quarterly figures.

[82] https://www.nytimes.com/2019/04/15/technology/cyberinsurance-notpetya-attack.html

Damage due to armed conflicts cannot be insured by law, due to the excessive financial risk. This causes few problems when war remains a distant prospect and there is a clear definition of 'armed conflict'. But cyber-attacks, which enable countries to harm each other's interests without ever setting foot on their soil, cannot be placed in this category so easily. A further question is whether and when computer code can be considered a 'weapon', particularly given the rapid evolution of malware. Most problematically, it is unclear when cyber-attacks merit retaliation; there are no international rules or definitions to determine this.[83] Now that insurers see cyber-attacks as a form of armed conflict and companies are protesting against this move, it is up to the legal system to determine the extent to which a cyber-attack carried out by a foreign state is, in fact, an act of war.[84]

The handling of other major incidents shows that solutions exist. After the 9/11 attacks, insurers withdrew because they no longer wanted to compensate clients for losses due to terrorist incidents. It is likewise almost impossible to insure against flooding in the Netherlands, although a public-private arrangement now provides insurance against terrorism, for which insurers are not required to compensate all losses and for which the government acts as the guarantor of last resort.[85] Similar public-private arrangements are found in Belgium and Germany. Such constructions enable insurers to offer insurance products without unacceptably high financial risks for themselves. Applied to digital disruption, it would mean that the government provides compensation for damages exceeding a certain limit. Once this guarantee has been provided, insurers could expand the market for cyber security risks and companies would, in principle, be liable for the costs of smaller incidents.

4.6 Conclusion

The government and other parties have always taken steps to minimize the potential consequences of societal disruption. Digitization adds a new form of disruption to the list of risks we are already familiar with. This section has focused on contingency measures in anticipation of digital disruption. Our main conclusion is that these measures have yet to be adequately implemented and that the government and other parties are insufficiently prepared. A number of steps are required:

- There is currently no coherent policy for critical infrastructure: for back-up options, the isolation of chains and networks, for cyber exercises, and for providing information on how to respond to urgent incidents. While regulations diverge between sectors and organizations, other factors undermine our preparedness as a society. Back-up options disappear as analogue systems are decommissioned

---

[83] Mačák, 2017.

[84] Several companies currently have legal cases against insurance companies, which may require judges to decide whether cyber-attacks are in fact a form of 'armed conflict'.

[85] For an extensive discussion of both attempts to insure against the risk of flooding and the terrorism pool, see Bruggeman & Faure, 2018: 61–62, 70–72.

and organizations outsource important facilities to third parties, further increasing the interdependence between processes and sectors.

- Information sharing has recently improved and become much more comprehensive. But it is still hampered by sectoral divisions and a partly outdated distinction between critical and non-critical providers. This means that signals may not be picked up (or picked up too late) by the relevant actors. A broader perspective is needed for gathering and sharing knowledge. While the current focus is on digital security measures, vulnerabilities and incidents, there is much less clarity for service providers and governments when it comes to chains, networks and the dependencies they create. This kind of knowledge is essential if we want to be able to classify the severity of incidents and manage the spread of digital disruption.

- In combating digital disruption, the government depends on information and cooperation from private actors (many of them based overseas). But the government lacks any clearly defined authority to intervene on the basis of specific categories of digital incidents; there is also little clarity about which public bodies should take action for which type of incident. Greater powers for the government should be accompanied by adequate protection for private parties, as interventions based on coercion may have adverse financial effects.

- Digital disruption can cross national borders, calling for international coordination. The current approach relies on partly inadequate national mechanisms, which is particularly risky in light of the spill-over effects into critical infrastructure elsewhere in Europe and attacks on European institutions. The need for European and international cooperation is urgent due to the geopolitical dynamics that surround digital disruption.

- Recovery and reconstruction would currently be difficult to achieve. The funds required for recovery would be in short supply now that insurers seem to be withdrawing from the cyber insurance market. But other major incidents of damage show that solutions are possible. While learning from incidents requires wide-ranging reflection and analysis, this is currently limited by various supervisory authorities processing the available data on incidents in isolation, precluding the benefits of potential learning effects.

References

AON. (2019). *Cyber perils in a growing market. Helping EMEA organizations better understand the interconnectivity among multiple lines of insurance.* https://www.aon.com/unitedkingdom/insights/cyber-perils-in-a-growing-market.jsp

Backman, S., & Rhinard, M. (2018). The European Union's capacities for managing crises. *Journal of Contingencies and Crisis Management, 26*(2), 261–271.

Bergström, J., Uhr, C., & Frykmer, T. (2016). A complexity framework for studying disaster response management. *Journal of Contingencies and Crisis Management, 24*(3), 124–135.

Bharosa, N., Lee, J., & Janssen, M. (2010). Challenges and obstacles in sharing and coordinating information during multi-agency disaster response: Propositions from field exercises. *Information Systems Frontiers, 12*(1), 49–65.

Biener, C., Eling, M., & Wirfs, J. H. (2015). Insurability of cyber risks: An empirical analysis. *Geneva Papers, 40*, 131–158.

Boeke, S. (2016). *First responder or last resort? The role of the ministry of defence in national cyber crisis management in four European Countries*. Leiden University.

Boin, R. A. (2017). *De grenzeloze crisis: Uitdagingen voor politiek en bestuur* [Crisis without borders: Challenges for politics and management]. Inaugural lecture, Leiden University.

Boin, R. A., & Lodge, M. (2018). *Enhancing the EU's transboundary crisis management capacity: Recommendations for practice*. TransCrisis.

Bruggeman, V., & Faure, M. (2018) Compensation for victims of disaster in Belgium, France, Germany and the Netherlands. *WRR Working Paper* 30. https://www.verzekeraars.nl/media/5662/compensation_for_victims_of_disasters_working_paper_30.pdf

Bulten, C., de Jong, B., Breukink, E., & Jettinghoff, A. (2017). *Vitale vennootschappen in veilige handen* [Vital companies in safe hands]. Radboud Business Law Institute. https://www.wodc.nl/binaries/2609_Volledige_Tekst_tcm28-250320.pdf

Carr, N. (2015). *De Glazen Kooi: Wat automatisering met ons doet* [The glass cage: What automation does to us]. Maven.

Cassa, C. A., Chunara, R., Mandl, K., & Brownstein, J. S. (2013). Twitter as a sentinel in emergency situations: Lessons from the Boston marathon explosions. *PLOS Currents Disasters*. https://currents.plos.org/disasters/index.html%3Fp=8687.html

CEPS (Centre for European Policy Studies). (2018). *Strengthening the EU's cyber defence capabilities. Report of a CEPS task force*. CEPS.

Choo, K. (2011). The cyber threat landscape: challenges and future research directions. *Computers & Security, 30*(8), 719–731.

Council for the Environment and Infrastructure. (2018). *Stroomvoorziening onder digitale spanning* [Electricity network under digital pressure]. The Hague.

CSR (Cyber Security Raad) [Cyber Security Council]. (2017). *Naar een landelijk dekkend stelsel van informatieknooppunten, advies inzake informatieuitwisseling met betrekking tot cybersecurity en cybercrime* [Towards a nationally comprehensive system on information nodes. Advice on information exchange regarding cyber security and cyber-crime]. https://www.cybersecurity-raad.nl/binaries/CSR_Advies_Informatieuitwisseling_NED_DEF_tcm107-314535.pdf

Donahue, A. K., Eckel, C. C., & Wilson, R. K. (2014). Ready or not? How citizens and public officials perceive risk and preparedness. *American Review of Public Administration, 44*(4), 89–111.

Dutch Safety Board. (2012). *Het DigiNotar-incident. Waarom digitale veiligheid de bestuurstafel te weinig bereikt* [The DigiNotar incident. Why digital security is not reaching the board room enough]. The Hague.

ENISA. (2015). *The 2015 report on national and international cyber security exercises. Survey, analysis and recommendations*. ENISA.

ENISA. (2017). *Commonality of risk assessment language in cyber insurance. Recommendations on cyber insurance*. https://www.enisa.europa.eu/publications/commonality-of-risk-assessment-language-in-cyber-insurance

ENISA. (2018). *Good practices on interdependencies between OES and DSPs*. ENISA.

EPSC [European Political Strategy Centre]. (2017). *Building an effective European Cyber Shield. Taking EU cooperation to the next level*. https://ec.europe.eu/epsc/publications/strategic-notes/building-effective-european-cyber-shield_en#-1

European Commission. (2016). *Strengthening Europe's cyber resilience system and fostering a competitive and innovative cybersecurity industry*. https://ec.europa.eu/transparency/regdoc/rep/1/2016/EN/1-2016-410-EN-F1-1.PDF

Frerks, G. (2018). Citizen engagement and resilience in Dutch disaster management: A black hole in *policy* and practise? In J. Bohland, J. Harrald, & D. Brosnan (Eds.), *The disaster resiliency challenge*. Charles C. Thomas.

Geer, D., Bace, R., Gutmann, P., Metzger, P., Pfleeger, C., Querterman, J., & Schneier, B. (2003). CyberInsecurity: The cost of monopoly – How the dominance of Microsoft's products poses a risk to security. *Computer & Communications Industry Association Report*. https://www.schneier.com/essays/archives/2003/09/cyberinsecurity_the.html

Greenberg, A. (2018). *The untold story of NotPetya, the most devastating cyberattack in history*. https://www.wired.com/story/notpetya-cyberattack-ukraine-russia-code-crashed-the-world/

Hausken, K. (2007). Information sharing among firms and cyber attacks. *Journal of Accounting and Public Policy, 26*(6), 639–688.

Helsloot, I., & Ruitenberg, A. (2004). Citizen response to disasters: A survey of literature and some practical implications. *Journal of Contingencies and Crisis Management, 12*(3), 98–111.

HM Government. (2016). *National cyber security strategy 2016–2021*. https://assets.publishing. service.gov.uk/government/uploads/system/uploads/attachment_data/file/567242/national_ cyber_security_strategy_2016.pdf

House of Lords. (2018). *Cyber security of the UK's critical national infrastructure*. https://publica-tions.parliament.uk/pa/jt201719/jtselect/jtnatsec/1708/1708.pdf

Inspectorate of Justice and Security. (2012). *Evaluatie van de rijkscrisisorganisatie tijdens de DigiNotar-crisis* [Evaluation of the national organizational crisis during the DigiNotar crisis]. The Hague.

Klaver, M. H. A., Verheesen, B., & Luiijf, H. A. M. (2013). *Intersectorale afhankelijkheden: buitenlandse methoden en mogelijke toepasbaarheid in Nederland* [Intersectoral dependencies: Methods from abroad and their possible application in the Netherlands]. TNO.

Koepke, P. (2017). *Cybersecurity information sharing incentives and barriers*. Sloan School of Management, MIT. https://cams.mit.edu/wp-content/uploads/2017-13.pdf

Kortmann, C. A. J. M. (2009). *Staatsrecht en raison d'État* [The rule of law and raison d'état]. Valedictory lecture, 27 February. Kluwer.

Kuipers, G. M., & Tjepkema, M. K. G. (2017). 'Public management' in Groningen. Publiekrechtelijke schadeafhandeling en het vertrouwen in de overheid [The settlement of pub-lic law claims and trust in the government]. *Nederlands Juristenblad, 29*(1576), 2058–2067.

Lawson, S. (2013). Beyond cyber-doom: Assessing the limits of hypothetical scenario's in the framing of cyber-threats. *Journal of Information Technology and Politics, 10*, 86–103.

Lloyd's and Cyence. (2017). *Counting the cost: Cyber exposure decoded*. Lloyd's.

Luiijf, E., & Kernkamp, A. (2015). *Sharing cyber security information: Good practice stemming from the Dutch public-private participation approach*. TNO.

Luiijf, E., & Klaver, M. (2015). Governing critical ICT: Elements that require attention. *European Journal of Risk Regulation, 2*(6), 263–270.

Mačák, K. (2017). From cyber norms to cyber rules: re-engaging states as law-makers. *Leiden Journal of International Law, 30*(4), 877–899.

Mueller, M. (2017). *Will the Internet Fragment? Sovereignty, Globalization and Cyberspace*. Polity Press.

Muller, E. R. (2014). Crisis en recht: Naar een integrale Crisisbeheersingswet? [Crisis and the law: Towards an integral Crisis Management Act?]. In E. R. Muller, T. Hartlief, B. F. Keulen, & H. Kummeling (Eds.), *Crises, rampen en recht* [Crisis, disasters and the law]. Kluwer.

NCTV. (2018). *Cybersecuritybeeld Nederland 2018* [Cyber security assessment Netherlands 2018]. NCTV.

NCTV. (2019). *Cybersecuritybeeld Nederland 2019* [Cyber security assessment Netherlands 2019]. NCTV.

Netherlands Court of Audit. (2019). *Digitale dijkverzwaring: Cybersecurity en vitale waterwerken* [Digital flood defences: Cyber security and vital defences]. The Hague.

Nieuwesteeg, B., Visscher, L., & de Waard, B. (2017). De rechtseconomie van cyberverzekeringen [The law and economics of cyber insurance]. *Het Verzekerings-archief, 3*, 155–160.

OECD. (2017). *Enhancing the role of insurance in cyber risk management*. OECD.

Overvest, B., Braam, A. M, Windig, R., & Bartels, E. (2018). *Knelpunten op de markt voor cyber-veiligheid* [Bottlenecks in the market for cyber security]. *CPB Policy Brief 2018/01*. CPB.

Prins, R. (2012). Een veilige cyberwereld vraagt nieuw denken [Safe cyber requires new thinking]. *Veiligheid in Cyberspace, Justitiële Verkenningen, 1*(12), 40–51.

Prins, J. E. J. (2019). Digitaal binnentreden om escalatie te voorkomen [Digital search warrants to prevent escalation]. *Nederlands Juristenblad, 578*.

Pupillo, L., Ferreiora, A., & Varisco, G. (2018). *Software vulnerability disclosure in Europe. Technology, policies and legal challenges*. Centre for European Policy Studies. https://www. ceps.eu/wp-content/uploads/2018/06/CEPS%20TFRonSVD%20with%20cover_0.pdf

Schneier, B. (2015). *Data and goliath: The hidden battles to collect your data and control your world*. W.W. Norton & Company.

Secrétariat général de la défense nationale. (2018). *Revue stratégique de cyberdéfense, 12 février 2018*. http://www.sgdsn.gouv.fr/uploads/2018/02/20180206-np-revue-cyber-public-v3.3-publication.pdf

Settanni, G., Skopik, F., Shovgenya, Y., Fiedler, R., Carolan, M., Conroy, D., et al. (2017). A collaborative cyber incident management system for European interconnected critical infrastructures. *Journal of Information Security and Applications, 34*, 166–182.

Simon, T., Goldberg, A., & Adini, B. (2015). Socializing in emergencies: a review of the use of social media in emergency situations. *International Journal of Information Management, 35*(5), 609–619.

Snyder, C. (2017). *Too connected to fail. How attackers can disrupt the global internet, why it matters and what we can do about It*. Cyber Security Project, Belfer Center for Science and International Affairs.

Valeriano, B., & Maness, R. C. (2018). How we stopped worrying about cyber doom and started collecting data. *Politics and Governance, 6*(2), 49–60.

Van Tiel, B. (2019). *Kritische waakhond, vergeet de digitale veiligheid niet* [Critical watch dog, do not forget digital security]. https://www.pwc.nl/nl/themas/blogs/kritische-waakhond-vergeet-de-digitale-veiligheid-niet.html

Van Vollenhoven. P. (2018). *Oproep van een waakhond* [Appeal from a watchdog]. Balans.

Ventsel, A., & Madisson, M. (2019). Semiotics of threats: Discourse on the vulnerability of the Estonian identity card. *Sign Systems Studies, 47*(1/2), 126–151.

WRR [Netherlands Scientific Council for Government Policy]. (2011a). *iOverheid* [iGovernment]. Amsterdam University Press. https://english.wrr.nl/latest/news/2011/11/29/igovernment-available-in-english

WRR [Netherlands Scientific Council for Government Policy]. (2011b). *Evenwichtskunst. Over de verdeling van verantwoordelijkheid voor fysieke veiligheid* [Balancing act. On the division of responsibility for physical security]. Amsterdam University Press. https://english.wrr.nl/latest/news/2012/10/09/evenwichtskunst-available-in-english

WRR [Netherlands Scientific Council for Government Policy]. (2012). *Publieke zaken in de marktsamenleving* [Public affairs in the market society]. Amsterdam University Press. https://www.wrr.nl/publicaties/rapporten/2012/04/12/publieke-zaken-in-de-marktsamenleving

WRR [Netherlands Scientific Council for Government Policy]. (2015). *De publieke kern van het internet. Naar een buitenlands internetbeleid* [The public core of the internet. Towards a foreign internet policy]. Amsterdam University Press. https://english.wrr.nl/publications/reports/2015/10/01/the-public-core-of-the-internet

WRR [Netherlands Scientific Council for Government Policy]. (2017). *Veiligheid in een wereld van verbindingen* [Security in a connected world]. WRR. https://www.springer.com/gp/book/9783030376055

Chapter 5
Conclusions and Recommendations

5.1 Introduction

On 24 June 2019, an hour-long outage hit the Dutch emergency number 112 and 0900–8844, the national police telephone line. It was also impossible to contact hospitals, municipalities, and companies for some time. The primary system of KPN – the telecom provider – was out of action while three back-up systems failed. The incident, which according to KPN was probably due to software error, once again revealed the vulnerability of facilities in the physical world to digital failures. It also underlined the report's central message: the need to be better prepared for incidents involving a digital dimension. These incidents are all the more critical when they are not limited to the digital domain, but have potentially disruptive consequences in the physical world and for confidence in the core institutions of society.

This incident in the Netherlands made it painfully clear how much the government depends on private parties for the continuity of critical processes, and how much these private parties depend on the services and facilities of external suppliers. Even more worryingly, the authorities, including the central government, were insufficiently prepared. There was no off-the-shelf emergency plan for an outage of the emergency number, while parties were unable to communicate to coordinate their response. It took 75 min before an alternative emergency number was distributed; an incorrect number was given out first, and not everyone received a notification from NL-Alert, the Dutch digital alarm system, on their mobile device. There had already been problems with the emergency number in 2012. The government minister responsible at the time had issued reassurances that this would not happen again. And yet it happened, showing that no system is 100% fail-safe. Apparently, even identical forms of disruption cannot be ruled out.

The previous sections focused on society's preparedness for digital disruption. We then analysed why the existing set of instruments does not adequately address such forms of disruption. In this concluding section, we offer suggestions for steps to improve our preparedness. These are intended for the government, particularly

© The Author(s) 2021
E. Schrijvers et al., *Preparing for Digital Disruption*, Research for Policy,
https://doi.org/10.1007/978-3-030-77838-5_5

for the national government. Since many other national governments around the world face similar challenges, our recommendations will, at least in some form, apply to them too. Sections 5.5.2 and 5.5.3 present our main conclusions. The subsequent sections contain our recommendations, which we discuss based on the four stages of preparedness, detection, mitigation, and recovery and reconstruction.

5.2 New Types of Disruption

The phenomenon of societal disruption has always been with us and can have a range of causes. Increasingly, the disruption or failure of digital services and facilities is one of these causes. This report has left aside questions about the likelihood and probable impact of digital disruption; such risk assessments are already available. As evidenced by numerous incidents in the Netherlands and elsewhere, the probability that digital disruption will occur is high enough to warrant planning how we will respond. The growing scale, spread and impact of digital incidents, their rising costs and economic implications, means that the trust that citizens, organizations and companies have in digital technologies is at stake.

Given the dependence on advanced digital technology across the breadth of our society and economy, the consequences of disruption go beyond the domain of 'traditional' information technology and cyber security. Digitization has blurred the distinction between the 'digital realm' and the 'physical realm'. The boundaries between companies and organizations – now interconnected by countless systems and networks – have become more diffuse. Digital disruption today means much more than the failure of isolated digital systems. This new reality, however, is not adequately acknowledged by companies, organizations, the government and politicians.

More and more societal and economic processes are based on interconnected flows of data and information. Developments such as 'datafication', the huge increase in the power and capabilities of computers, and the complex web of interconnections between systems around the world mean that the physical realm is now inextricably bound up with the digital realm. Virtually all of society's core processes – including our power supply, the processing of payments, flood defences and healthcare systems – now depend on the exchange of data and digital systems linked to wider networks including the internet. Interdependence is therefore built-in and must be considered, both when preparing for and combating incidents that involve our digital infrastructure. It is no longer sufficient to leave the implementation of protection measures to individual organizations, or for them to practise responding to cyber incidents within their own company or sector. The weakest link in the chain, which could allow an incident to occur, could be almost anywhere in the world.

Digitization is changing the scale and dynamics of disruptive incidents. This is due not only to the highly interconnected nature of digital infrastructure, but to the use of unsafe, generic software and hardware, network dependencies, and the sometimes inadequate protection of systems and data. Complex, often opaque and cross-border production and supply chains provide malicious actors with myriad opportunities to disrupt social and economic processes, or even to bring them to a halt. Digital disruption can occur at lightning speed, affecting a large number of organizations and sectors around the world; it can also result from dormant processes that go unnoticed for long periods of time or are unclear in scope. Both may shake confidence in our state institutions, democracy and constitution, as members of society perceive the government has insufficient control over the digital realm. If disruption strikes, it is not clear in advance whether it is the government's responsibility to take action, and if so, which part of government. And yet, a swift response may be required to limit the damage.

Digitization has in many ways undermined the relevance of geographical borders. Numerous incidents have shown that problems can simultaneously lead to disruption in many countries. Digital disruption must therefore be addressed by international bodies, including the European Union. But cross-border digitization does not mean that individual countries have no role in addressing its attendant threats. Some disruptions are limited to the national level, such as the disruption of KPN's telephone system in the Netherlands. One key lesson is that digital disruption – however abstract it may seem – will ultimately always have local consequences. Finally, for contingency measures from fall-back options and disconnection scenarios to insurance and compensation, individual countries depend on other nations. In short, preparedness for digital disruption must combine national measures with international cooperation and coordination.

5.3 Centralized Setting of Standards and Coordination by Government

In security policy, the government is expected to clarify what interests are at stake. It needs to clarify how costs, benefits, and risks are distributed in light of these interests, and which parties bear responsibility for what.[1] Extending this line of reasoning, government must play a greater role in the digital domain and in addressing its associated risks.

This role requires explanation. A centralized system of management for cyber security, internet governance and critical infrastructure – populated largely by private actors – is unrealistic. But the government can play its role in other ways. Over the past decade, cyber security has emerged as a serious international policy field. Public-private partnerships have become indispensable, especially now that most of our digital infrastructure is in private hands. This collaboration, however, is largely free of legal obligations. Providers of critical services are largely free to determine their own protection measures and back-up and fall-back options; their preparedness for digital disruption varies considerably. They also have great latitude in

---

[1] WRR, 2011.

reporting incidents, while active participation in the Information Sharing Analysis Centres is mainly limited to the select group of organizations that have acknowledged the importance of sharing information.

Private companies and organizations cannot be expected to assume full responsibility for digital disruption. But when it does occur, they can be expected to do everything in their powers to prevent the situation from deteriorating further. While the government is, by definition, best placed to enforce this responsibility, it now only has a limited set of instruments to do so. Should private organizations and companies refuse to cooperate in the event of disruption (or imminent disruption), the central government has relatively limited powers to force cooperation. This is even more the case at the European level, as the EU is limited to an advisory role and the strategic and operational aspects of cyber are the responsibility of the member states. Clarifying and strengthening the powers available to government as well as standards for intervention[2] would enhance the government's capacity to act in the event of digital disruption.

Nevertheless, the starting point must be that local 'fire brigades' take care of local fires and specialist fire brigades take care of more complex fires at the local, regional or national levels. After all, different measures will often be required in each domain. If there is a risk of digital disruption, escalation to a higher administrative level can be considered and central government can decide to take the lead in crisis management. The division of responsibilities for digital incidents remains unclear in many countries. Partly because there are no criteria to distinguish between different categories of incidents, there are no mechanisms in place for how and when higher authorities step in.

The threat of digital disruption requires coordinated action from government. Due to both network effects and the interaction between the digital and physical realms, contingency plans must transcend individual organizations. It is virtually impossible for any organization, company or safety region to have a comprehensive picture, let alone enough information to make the right decisions about the deactivation of networks, escalation, or the many other urgent measures that may be required. An overview of the coherence of processes, of the dependencies involved, and of the measures to be taken requires coordinated action by government. So does providing the right public information when things go wrong. The government also remains responsible for existing resources in the field of cyber security.[3]

Better preparedness by the government cannot be a license for other actors to take unnecessary risks. Companies and organizations have their share of responsibility in preparing for digital disruption. If they fail to act on their responsibilities, this may undermine public confidence in digital processes, which in the long run will adversely affect the functioning of society, market and government. Even if only one party decides that preparatory measures are not worth the bother, all will be affected when things go wrong.

---

[2] Cf. Boeke, 2016

[3] Such as the public information provided on https://crisis.nl/wees-voorbereid/cyberaanval/. Suggestions for cyber-attacks are limited to 'digital' measures such as changing passwords and installing new antivirus software. In the event of a multi-day failure of the national card payment system, citizens would benefit more from advice to keep cash ready for emergencies.

Some measures are already in place to coordinate our preparedness for digital disruption. For example, parties who fail to take precautions to limit adverse effects, or who do so inadequately, can in some cases be held liable.[4] But there is plenty of scope for improvement among private-sector actors, such as organizing cyber exercises and drills for disruption in light of network effects and dependence on external parties. Companies and organizations could also be required to include a section on cyber security in their annual reports, focusing on preparatory measures and precautions. A number of our recommendations concern the private sector.

5.4   Focusing on Preparedness

Governments have long been protecting the infrastructure necessary for society's continuity. This requires an understanding of how particular infrastructures are vulnerable to disruption, failure or destruction. While anyone familiar with these vulnerabilities can take precautionary measures to minimize the consequences of disruptive events, at present not enough is being done.

This report is underpinned by the conviction that the possibility of digital disruption is not being taken seriously enough. The current policy focus on prevention and protection is too limited and could have grave consequences. First, there has been no public or political debate about which facilities are essential to ensure cyber security in the Netherlands, or about the most effective approach to take in the event of digital disruption. Our first recommendation is therefore:

> To initiate a public debate about the preparedness of Dutch society for digital disruption.

Digitization increasingly determines the vulnerability of core societal processes. Public debate is needed about how much 'strategic autonomy' is desirable and feasible for an individual nation state. While digitization leads to faster and more efficient processes, incidents can quickly affect multiple organizations, sectors and countries. What is the right balance between the advantages and disadvantages of digitization? If things go wrong, what fall-back options should be available? How long can a disruption reasonably last? What recovery time would we find acceptable?

Market developments affect the preparedness of society and government. Investment decisions, corporate take-overs and network effects in the digital world result in dependencies which can be difficult to mitigate. These dependencies can also hinder the government's implementation of its own safety measures. An important question is therefore which facilities or companies we wish to keep within our own jurisdictions in order to protect the national and/or European interest. The

---

[4] Van Dam, 1995; Keirse, 2017

implications of relying on overseas actors and entities for the effectiveness of our approach to digital disruption should be given more weight in this discussion.

More than is currently the case, governments will need to build up the knowledge required to identify the risks of this new reality early on, and to formulate policies on digital disruption. This would entail evaluation of how far we wish to have fall-back options available, such as the ability to isolate systems and facilities so that they can continue to function offline.[5]

5.5   Detection: A Clearer Picture of Dependencies

Preparedness and problem detection are closely intertwined. We need a clearer picture of the dependencies between the digital and physical realms, and within specific sectors of society. This will require greater efforts from government. We need to revisit the list of critical infrastructure as what we have now is insufficiently attuned to the realities of the digital world. How we prioritize critical processes will have to be reviewed.

5.5.1   Insight into Dependencies

Detecting digital disruption at an early stage will require detailed understanding of the connections between cyber and physical sectors. It will also require better insight into the chains and networks – indispensable for the core processes of society – within which Dutch and other national and international organizations operate. We need to know who owns, or is allowed to own, shares in these organizations, and who has formal or effective control over shareholders.[6] We need a more comprehensive overview of various sectors – including their possible dominance by particular service providers – and the jurisdictions in which key providers and other players are based to facilitate international consultation should rapid measures be necessary. In the absence of such knowledge, risks cannot be rigorously evaluated, information on incidents cannot be properly interpreted, and our preparations for digital disruption will fall short. Our second recommendation is therefore to:

> Conduct an assessment of cyber dependencies focusing on the parties, digital elements, processes and services essential for the functioning of critical processes in society.

---

[5] Cf. WRR, 2017: 67–77, 186.
[6] Bulten et al., 2017.

Such a 'dependency assessment' will augment cyber security assessments by various countries that annually review major incidents, threats, interests and resilience.[7] Given the sensitivity of the information, the details should not be published. What matters is that the information is used to better understand incidents and decisions, both before and during episodes of disruption. The information can also be used to inform strategic discussions and choices about how far social and economic provisions in the country depend on specific actors.

Our recommendation to conduct a cyber-dependency assessment refers specifically to companies and organizations involved in critical processes. Other companies and organizations can of course conduct such assessments as well, particularly if they play key roles in the functioning of society, for example hospitals, distribution services and payment platforms. Keeping abreast of evolving dependencies is primarily the responsibility of private companies, public services and individual organizations; they will need to periodically refresh their knowledge in light of economic and technological developments. While exercises for scenarios involving digital disruption are an obvious tool, they remain rare and may need to become mandatory, certainly for critical infrastructure.

At the same time, preparation for digital disruption will have to transcend the capacities of individual organizations. Even where parties have detailed knowledge of their own dependencies, the wider picture for the sector and interrelationships with other domains may be much less clear. The entire public sector should be involved to yield a more comprehensive picture. For example, we know that many companies and organizations depend on the cloud services of just two major US providers: Microsoft and Amazon. The same applies to reliance on suppliers of industrial control systems, electronic patient records and ATMs. But we do not know enough about the sum of these dependencies or their significance for particular organizations and sectors, or even for the country as a whole. This also applies to the question of exactly what processes are at stake. We need to know more about the wider context to be able to identify risks and to prepare for disruption.

5.5.2 A New Approach to the Identification of Critical Infrastructure

A comprehensive overview of dependencies would provide a better understanding of which organizations require a higher level of protection and government support, including the sharing of information about risks. In many countries, these organizations are based on lists of critical infrastructure. These lists are invaluable; their exact composition is a key determinant of how well countries are prepared for digital disruption.

---

[7] Most recently: https://www.ncsc.nl/onderwerpen_a_z/csbn/index.aspx

The selection of critical processes is politically challenging, partly because protecting them is costly and the government often has no direct control over the parties involved. The current 'system' works primarily to the benefit of the central government and those organizations designated as critical providers. Parties not on the list need to make their own arrangements. In a highly networked world, this has undeniable consequences, both nationally and internationally, not least for those parties designated as constituting critical infrastructure.

The first reason to revisit our current list of critical infrastructure is the increasingly crucial role of digital processes in society. This includes stand-alone digital services such as electronic message traffic and authentication as well as processes that support other critical functions such as the supply of electricity and payment traffic. Although some have been added to the list of critical infrastructures in recent years, the question is whether this is sufficient. Due to the rapid development and wide adoption of digital applications in many areas of society, new and significant vulnerabilities arise unexpectedly, requiring the inclusion of new organizations as providers of critical services. An example is the payment service Facebook is planning to launch.

Second, we need to examine whether it remains useful to link critical processes to individual providers. There is ample reason to believe that identifying the chains and networks that support critical processes – meaning all those parties that providers of the service depend on – would yield better results. This might mean that actors other than the direct providers of critical services should also be categorized as critical infrastructure. In short, the policy on critical processes will need to clarify how actors deemed 'critical' fit into the relevant chain or network, based on the principle that some components are indispensable for the continuity of a given critical process. The example of the electricity supply (discussed in Sect. 5.4) shows that incidents that affect actors not classified as critical providers can contribute to disruption through cascade effects. If an incident outside of the critical sector is not addressed in time, the critical infrastructure itself may be affected.

The cross-border nature of many chains and networks has implications for European harmonization in the protection of critical infrastructure. Greater focus is required at the European level on the links between providers designated as critical, between themselves and with external parties. At the same time, greater commitment is required from EU member states. The different ways in which countries govern critical sectors and the services covered by the Network and Information Security Directive make it difficult to work together to identify and mitigate cross-border incidents and those that affect European networks and institutions. For example, while the NIS Directive includes measures for the healthcare sector, the Netherlands did not include healthcare when implementing the Directive in its legislation on network and information systems security (the WBNI). This means that, in the event of an incident, there is no common point of contact for member states in the field of healthcare. Such omissions hamper the creation of a Europe-wide system for the entire system of critical infrastructure.

Operationalize critical infrastructure differently, starting with the chains and networks that support critical processes.

Examine whether digitization requires changes to the prioritization of critical processes.

5.5.3 Digital Triage

In the Netherlands, the list of critical processes – last reviewed in 2014 – includes criteria for prioritization in case of disruption. On the basis of various impact criteria, the list distinguishes between two categories of critical processes, prioritizing those with the greatest impact – due to for instance cascade effects – should they fail. While prioritization can limit damage and promote swift recovery, we need to review the existing categorization of critical processes in light of digitization. We refer to this prioritization process as 'digital triage'.[8] Even where, as in many other countries, no distinctions are drawn between critical processes, their digitization requires revisiting which ones to prioritize in case of disruption.

The question is whether the current system is adequate given our growing dependence on digital technology. The prioritization of critical processes based on 'impact' may also need revisiting; in a crisis situation, the most important processes for a rapid recovery may be quite different from those that have the greatest impact. The continuity of many critical processes depends on digital facilities and services, which may warrant higher priority as they facilitate the restoration of other important societal functions. Digital communication facilities in particular may deserve higher priority as they play a key role in keeping citizens informed and in preventing or containing social unrest.

Digital triage based on this dual perspective – including both impact and recovery options – would, in the event of a crisis, enable ministers to take decisions that have already been discussed and accepted in advance. During a disruptive event, there may not be time for any reflective decision-making. Such a system of triage would mean that the parties involved are informed in advance; they would not be taken by surprise and would be able to act more quickly. This would ultimately improve the resilience of society's critical functions.[9]

As the Dutch government's dependence on Microsoft during the DigiNotar incident revealed, it is an illusion to think that the government is the only key actor in this area. Other actors often participate in the decision-making necessary to combat

---

[8] The term 'triage' comes from the French verb *trier*, meaning to rank. Its usage can be traced to the work of field nurses in Napoleon's army, who developed a method of evaluating injuries and evacuating patients following battle (Baker, 2007). The concept has been applied to cyber security analysts detecting and monitoring networks (Ben-Asher & Gonzalez, 2015; Zhong et al., 2018). The digital triage we propose extends beyond the digital domain to identifying priorities when restoring vital societal processes in a digitizing society.

[9] Verner et al., 2017

digital disruption and to enable swift recovery. Good communication channels with these parties is essential to guarantee the continued functioning of society during a crisis. The assessment of dependencies discussed above would be useful here.

5.6   Mitigation: More Powers, Better Categorization of Incidents and Better European Coordination

If things go wrong unexpectedly, the government must be able to bring the situation under control. But as things currently stand, the government would face several problems. First, there is no equivalent to the familiar emergency services model in our new digitized reality. Second, there is no clear categorization of incidents that outlines when the relevant authorities and actors should become involved. Third, dealing with disruptive events with a cross-border or European dimension are hampered by lack of coordination.

5.6.1   Legal Powers and Competencies

When digital disruption threatens societal disruption, the government must have the right information at its disposal and be ready to act. Action may have to be far-reaching. During the DigiNotar incident in 2011, the Dutch government stepped in because the extent of the problem was unclear and confidence in its own digital services was at stake. Unfortunately, the government's actions during the DigiNotar incident were never evaluated. The question of which powers the government actually needs has therefore never been properly debated – an important conversation to have as the government can now only legally provide advice and assistance. This means that organizations and companies are not obliged to follow the government's advice when dealing with digital disruption, and may decide to pursue priorities that conflict with the public interest. Where organizations and companies are not part of the critical infrastructure, the government is largely powerless.

Although the government has a range of options for intervening based on existing crisis management legislation, there is no specific focus on how it should handle digital disruption. Current crisis decision-making is organized along functional lines or linked to a particular municipality, region or the central government. Although the central government can always intervene in the event of an emergency, it would be preferable if interventions occurred in a predictable and controlled manner, particularly if it concerns the police or the public prosecution service. A crucial question is whether such interventions would be justifiable if they did not also serve the purposes of an investigation or prosecution. After all, we rightly expect the fire brigade to extinguish the fire, not to confiscate our household effects. In a digitized world, this distinction becomes more difficult to draw because data does not need to be removed to be reused for other purposes. Our recommendation is therefore to:

Provide a clearly defined legal mandate for a digital taskforce responsible for combating (potential) digital disruption that could have adverse effects on society. As part of this, examine the need for separate regulations for government action to prevent incidents from escalating and for categorizing incidents.

Generic, legally established powers, accompanied by an appropriate framework, would give the government more freedom to act to combat digital disruption. The aim should be to safeguard citizens and businesses from disproportionate, uncontrolled or arbitrary acts on the part of government.[10] Such a framework would be particularly important if there is a risk of disruption but the effects cannot yet be discerned.

5.6.2 Towards a Categorization of Incidents

In elaborating the government's legal powers, it would be preferable to specify them on the basis of different categories of digital incidents. Such a system is already in place in the United States, France and the United Kingdom. Not all categories of incidents disrupt critical processes or represent a threat to national security. A more detailed system of categorization would facilitate assessing the potential consequences of an incident, the need to use special powers, and the decision to deploy a particular organization to take action. Differentiation according to the seriousness of situations could also prevent the central government from becoming involved too quickly. An effective system of categorization would provide opportunities for administrative and political escalation. Our response to fires is essentially decentralized; escalating the response is possible when the magnitude of the incident requires it.

5.6.3 European Coordination

Given the cross-border nature of digital disruption, the recommendations outlined above for combating incidents should be on the international agenda as well. The European Union is an obvious starting point, now that the NIS Directive provides for greater uniformity in the protection of service providers in critical processes. To effectively combat digital disruption, individual countries will often depend on cooperation from foreign governments. Other countries will also ask it for assistance.

Individual EU member states can contribute to a more coordinated approach at the European level by bolstering the NIS cooperation group.[11] The NIS cooperation group was established as part of the implementation of the NIS Directive and is

---

[10] WRR, 2016: 97.

[11] https://ec.europa.eu/digital-single-market/en/nis-cooperation-group

supported by the national Computer Security Incident Response Teams (CSIRTs), the European Commission and the ENISA agency. Like the European Article 29 Working Group, which has since been succeeded by the legally constituted European Data Protection Board,[12] this partnership could eventually serve as a stepping stone towards an organization with greater legal competencies at the EU level. Those competencies should focus on combating incidents that affect European institutions or that transcend the capacities of individual member states to such an extent that they pose risks to critical infrastructure elsewhere in Europe.[13]

5.7   Recovery & Reconstruction: Examine the Possibility of a Cyber Pool and Make Better Use of Data on Incidents

A disruptive event is often followed by a period of recovery and reconstruction. A range of issues will need to be addressed, from support and compensation for victims to evaluating what went wrong. We recommend adding two further issues to the agenda relevant to recovery after a major incident. First, we should look closely at the feasibility of establishing a cyber pool for compensating damages. Second, we can learn how to better use the available data on incidents.

5.7.1   Cyber Pool

An important aspect of recovery and reconstruction is compensating victims in the form of liability or compensation payments, whether through insurance or through government payments.[14] The aim of such instruments is to enable parties that suffer damage to resume normal functioning wherever possible and, preferably, to return to their previous positions. The reality is often different, if only because countless questions arise about the attribution and causes of the damage or, for example, at which moment the damage should be assessed.[15]

Liability, compensation and insurability are difficult to design and regulate in a digitizing world. Cascade effects, complex interactions between information processes, and associated questions over causality are bound to play a role. Perpetrators are often never found, and there is a high level of uncertainty about both the risks

---

[12] https://edpb.europa.eu/

[13] Compare with the proposal for a European cyber agency in CEPS 2018. This agency also has the authority to attribute attacks.

[14] Alongside compensation for actors that have suffered damages, civil liability may also play a role in (and serve as an alternative to) public law measures designed to ensure better preparedness. Organizations that have to foot the bill themselves will be more inclined to minimize costs and to be better prepared.

[15] Hartlief, 2014.

and the types of cost that may be involved. As explained in Sect. 4.5, insurability is an urgent issue. Insurance is essentially a matter for the market. But where there are market failures and risks cannot be hedged adequately, the government can try to provide people with more peace of mind.

The government could make insurance compulsory by law – admittedly often a long process seen as interventionist. The government could also create a reinsurance fund with other actors to ensure that risks are insurable. Such insurance 'pools' – where each party participates at a predetermined percentage – are often used to insure major or technically complex risks. Now that insurers seem to be withdrawing from the market for cyber insurance due to fears of excessive claims, a 'cyber pool' construction warrants further study. As a possible template, the Dutch Reinsurance Company for Terrorist Damage insures all sectors for damage up to €1 billion per calendar year, to be provided by national insurers, international reinsurers and the Dutch state.[16] In 2003, the Netherlands led the way internationally with this construction.

> Explore the feasibility of a national or European 'cyber pool' arrangement in order to provide insurance cover for the financial damage caused by digital disruption.

As part of this exploration, identifying and quantifying 'systemic risks' deserves special attention. Insurers, large utility companies, banks, multinationals, and governments around the world are increasingly turning to quantitative models to manage cyber risks. Although this is a step in the right direction, there are as yet no reliable methods for identifying systemic risks – a fluid and complex category of risk that goes beyond the level of individual organizations. The government could contribute to the development of more reliable methods through steps such as making its knowledge and data available to other parties.

It is also important to determine whether cyber-attacks can be regarded as armed conflict under international law and, if so, to what extent and which types of cyber-attack. As we discussed in Sect. 4.5, this is crucial for the insurability of damage caused by cyber-attacks. In order not to unnecessarily obstruct the development of a mature cyber-insurance market, national governments should take a cautious approach to characterizing cyber-attacks as acts of war.

5.7.2   Make Better Use of Data on Incidents

Recovery and particularly reconstruction provide opportunities to be better prepared for the next incident and to re-evaluate which interests should be given priority. Learning from past decisions and mistakes plays an important role; learning

---

[16] Bruggeman & Faure, 2018: 70–72, 82.

from minor incidents can prevent much larger and more disruptive events in the future.

While improving our capacity for collective learning can take numerous forms, internal and external supervision would be useful.[17] External supervisors, who now receive and process incident reports including reports on problems with the continuity of core processes, have valuable data at their disposal. A necessary step towards improving our capacity for learning is to gather and make more systematic use of the information available to supervisory bodies. Supervisors are important nodes of information, well positioned to learn general lessons from series of minor incidents and to make this information available more widely. While the legally required reports on data breaches, disruptions and continuity problems are currently received by various supervisory authorities, the information in these reports is rarely analysed systematically. As a result, supervisory authorities are depriving themselves, and the parties they supervise, of valuable information that could be used to improve our level of preparedness for digital disruption. Such information could include insights into likely types of perpetrators for specific kinds of attacks.

> Ensure that information on incidents is available at the national and European levels; make better use of this information; and provide effective feedback to the parties involved in order to strengthen the capacity for collective learning.

We need to make better use of the data generated through the NIS Directive's reporting obligations. The Directive specifically aims to ensure greater coherence in the cyber security policy of European member states; for this to succeed, governments must make greater efforts to ensure that data on incidents is better shared and analysed at the European level. This task could be assigned to the NIS cooperation group.

5.8   Closing Words

Often without our noticing it, digital infrastructure has become intertwined with processes essential to the continuity of our society, economy, democracy and the rule of law. In the coming years, this relationship will become ever closer due to developments such as artificial intelligence, cloud computing and the Internet of Things. It is laudable that the protection of digital infrastructure is receiving more attention. At the same time, 100% security can never be guaranteed. In addition to existing policy, this report has therefore presented the case for better preparedness

---

[17] WRR, 2013: 150, 155.

for situations in which digital infrastructure is disrupted or out of action, and there is a risk of societal disruption as a result.

There is too much at stake to leave preparing for digital disruption to chance. The extent of our reliance on digital infrastructure means that measures must be taken to limit potential damage and to ensure that affected parties can recover as quickly as possible. Within existing frameworks, the government is hampered in its ability to adequately deal with digital disruption; its traditional set of instruments to address societal disruption are insufficient for this purpose. The recommendations in this section provide a range of options for new ways of doing things. Their implementation will require a thorough consideration of the role and responsibilities of government in a digitizing world.

References

Baker, M. S. (2007). Creating order from chaos. Part I: Triage, initial care, and tactical considerations in mass casualty and disaster response. *Military Medicine, 172*(3), 232–236.

Ben-Asher, N., & Gonzalez, C. (2015). Effects of cyber security knowledge on attack detection. *Computers in Human Behavior, 48*, 51–61.

Boeke, S. (2016). *First responder or last resort? The role of the ministry of defence in national cyber crisis management in four European countries*. Leiden University.

Bruggeman, V., & Faure, M. (2018). Compensation for victims of disaster in Belgium, France, Germany and the Netherlands. *WRR Working Paper* 30. https://www.verzekeraars.nl/media/5662/compensation_for_victims_of_disasters_working_paper_30.pdf

Bulten, C., de Jong, B., Breukink, E., & Jettinghoff, A. (2017). *Vitale vennootschappen in veilige handen* [Vital companies in safe hands]. Radboud Business Law Institute. https://www.wodc.nl/binaries/2609_Volledige_Tekst_tcm28-250320.pdf

CEPS (Centre for European Policy Studies). (2018). *Strengthening the EU's cyber defence capabilities. Report of a CEPS task force*. CEPS (Centre for European Policy Studies).

Hartlief, T. (2014). Privaatrecht in nood – Over de beperkte betekenis van het privaatrecht bij rampen en crises en een rechtsgebied onder toenemende druk van het publiekrecht [Private law in need – on the limited usefulness of private law in the event of disasters and crises and increasing pressure on this field of law from public law]. In E. R. Muller, T. Hartlief, B. F. Keulen, & H. Kummeling (Eds.), *Crises, rampen en recht* [Crises, disasters and the law]. Kluwer.

Keirse, A. L. M. (2017). Rechtsvergelijkend perspectief: staatsaansprakelijkheid voor onrechtmatige rechtspraak in de lidstaten [Comparative law perspective: state liability for unlawful jurisdiction in the member states]. *Overheid en Aansprakelijkheid, 2017*(2), 81–90.

Van Dam, C. C. (1995). Aansprakelijkheid voor nalaten [Liability for negligence]. *Preadvies voor de Nederlandse Vereniging voor Rechtsvergelijking* [Preliminary advice for the Netherlands Comparative Law Association]. Kluwer.

Verner, D., Petit, F., & Kim, K. (2017). Incorporating prioritization in critical infrastructure security and resilience programs. *Homeland Security Affairs, 13*. https://www.hsaj.org/articles/14091

WRR [Netherlands Scientific Council for Government Policy]. (2011). *Evenwichtskunst. Over de verdeling van verantwoordelijkheid voor fysieke veiligheid* [Balancing act. On the division of responsibility for physical security]. Amsterdam University Press. [link toevoegen]

WRR [Netherlands Scientific Council for Government Policy]. (2013). *Toezien op publieke belangen. Naar een verruimd perspectief op rijkstoezicht* [Supervising in the public interest. Towards a broader perspective on government supervision]. Amsterdam University Press. [link toevoegen]

WRR [Netherlands Scientific Council for Government Policy]. (2016). *Big data in een vrije en veilige samenleving* [Big data in a free and safe society]. Amsterdam University Press.

WRR [Netherlands Scientific Council for Government Policy]. (2017). *Veiligheid in een wereld van verbindingen* [Security in a connected world]. WRR. [link toevoegen]

Zhong, C., Lin, T., Liu, P., Yen, J., & Chen, K. (2018). A cyber security data triage operation retrieval system. *Computers & Security, 76*, 12–31.

Printed in the United States
by Baker & Taylor Publisher Services